A DOG
NAMED JUDY

FRANK DETER, JR.

SUNBURY
PRESS

Mechanicsburg, Pennsylvania   USA

Published by Sunbury Press, Inc.
50 West Main Street
Mechanicsburg, Pennsylvania 17055

SUNBURY
PRESS

www.sunburypress.com

For information about special discounts for bulk purchases, please contact Sunbury Press Orders Dept. at (855) 338-8359 or orders@sunburypress.com.

To request one of our authors for speaking engagements or book signings, please contact Sunbury Press Publicity Dept. at publicity@sunburypress.com.

ISBN: 978-1-62006-609-6 (hardcover)

Library of Congress Control Number: 2015944696

FIRST SUNBURY PRESS EDITION: June 2015

Product of the United States of America
0 1 1 2 3 5 8 13 21 34 55

Set in Bookman Old Style
Designed by Lawrence Knorr
Cover by Lawrence Knorr
Cover Art by Marcia Welch
Edited by Taylor Berger-Knorr

Continue the Enlightenment!

DEDICATION

To My Beloved Son,
Frank Deter, III.
May we hunt together, again,
with Judy one day.

TABLE OF CONTENTS

PROLOGUE

Once in the lifetime of an exceptionally fortunate hunter and gun dog owner, an extraordinary dog is born and comes into his possession.

This is a true story of one such dog, from the advent of her birth until her last hunt and beyond. The dog was a charming little female beagle to which her owner; the author of this book, and his son and daughter; gave the name "Judy."

In the beginning, the man's goal was to provide his young son with the opportunity to begin his lifelong hunting experience in the company of a thoroughbred hunting dog. He wanted nothing more than the fledgling hunter and the dog to grow and mature together; intensifying the bond between them.

As the story unfolds, Judy becomes a loving member of the man's family, and begins to show promise as an exceptional gun dog. With each unforgettable hunt, the man's goal draws nearer to attainment, as Judy far exceeds his expectations. As he and his son comb the fields and woodlands together with Judy on crisp autumn mornings, and on winter days with the hills and valleys white with snow, they build treasured memories that will remain with them throughout their lives.

Throughout his formative years, the man's son enjoyed the character-strengthening experience of close association with respected and accomplished friends of his father. On many occasions, those friends accompanied his father and him on days in the forests and fields with Judy, and cast a lasting influence of high standards upon the young, novice hunter.

By all those who shared the privilege of venturing afield with Judy, seasoned hunters and novices alike, she was proclaimed an outstanding gun dog. She was one which overshadowed her peers, and one which was widely sought after, but rarely emerges from her breed. She was a beloved and treasured member of the man's family, and she will live in their memories eternally.

The names of the man's family members and relatives mentioned in this book are authentic. The names of two of the characters included in the story, Guido Malacarne and Joe Pesi, are also authentic. Throughout the man's entire life, Guido and Joe have been, and remain to this day, two of his closest and most respected friends.

The names of all other characters mentioned, described, or referred to, have been substituted, since most are long deceased. At the time of this writing, the author had no knowledge of the whereabouts of their next of kin. The names given are fictitious, and are therefore a product of the author's imagination. Any resemblance to persons living or dead is purely coincidental.

CHAPTER I
THE QUEST FOR JUDY

I spent the years of my boyhood in the village of Reynoldsville the heart of the western Pennsylvania coal region, and where rabbit hunting with beagles was a way of life. As the brilliant splendor of autumn gave way to the shedding of leaves, and the cry of the southbound Canada geese was a frequent sound, the hills surrounding my boyhood home came alive with the sound of beagle music and the sharp reports of the hunters' guns.

As one passed through the streets of town, a typical Pennsylvania beagle kennel, with an elevated wire mesh run attached to a wooden weather shelter could be seen in the backyards of many homes. When the noon fire

3

whistle blew, a howling chorus heard for miles around would follow.

I grew up at my grandparents' home at the edge of town with my Aunt Lois and Uncle Pat who also lived there. We kept thoroughbred beagles from the time of my early youth. One of my duties was to feed and care for them, which I carried out most willingly in anticipation of the day when I'd reach the age of twelve and could legally be a licensed hunter.

In the years before I was old enough to obtain a license, when the opening day of rabbit season arrived and the hunters would take to the thickets and fields, my grandmother would give me strict orders to stay out of the woods. Against her wishes, I would sneak off to the wooded areas near our home, accompanied by my mixed-breed dog, "Elmer," and with my trusty single-shot air rifle in hand. My desire to hunt overshadowed the prospect of Grandmother's wrath.

By his markings and his eagerness to hunt, one could readily tell that Elmer was part beagle. But, he lacked the beagle's intense sense of smell. He worked his way into the thickets with all the enthusiasm of a thoroughbred, but when the rabbit was routed, he was unable to pursue it by the scent left on the ground, and could take up the chase by sight only.

When the opportunity for a clear shot was presented, I would shoot at the rabbit. I scored many hits, but my air rifle lacked the power for a kill. Consequently, I succeeded only in causing the rabbit to increase its speed in making its way to the safety of another thicket.

When finally the day came that I was old enough to purchase my first hunting license, I began to hunt with my uncles and other men in our neighborhood who owned thoroughbred dogs.

For the first two years, I hunted with a .410 gauge single-shot gun, which was a birthday gift from my family. I was surprisingly successful with my little .410, and brought much game home for the dinner table. I graduated to a 12 gauge gun at about the age of fourteen, which increased my range and therefore my success.

My Aunt Lois and Uncle Pat were much more than just my aunt and uncle.

At the time of my birth, my mother and father lived in Batavia, a small suburb of Cincinnati, Ohio. In my infancy, my mother died, and my grandmother dispatched Aunt Lois to travel by train to Batavia, and to bring me to the old home in Reynoldsville. With the assistance and admonishments of my grandmother, Aunt Lois and Uncle Pat raised me as their own.

Uncle Pat and Aunt Lois, whom I began to call "Ma" at a very early age, were very loving and devoted substitute parents. As I look back upon my early years, I'm certain that no natural mother and father could have been more devoted to the responsibilities of parenthood.

Uncle Pat and I shared countless happy times together on trout streams, hunting with our beagles, and other forms of companionship. I've always thought he was the most unselfish man who ever lived. Literally everything he did was for the benefit of someone else. "Ma," of course, shared his virtues, to my good fortune. To our overwhelming loss and to the misfortune of all those whose lives he touched, Uncle Pat was stricken with an incurable cancer and passed away at an early age.

After graduation from high school at the age of eighteen, I left home to serve four years in the United States Marine Corps. Soon after my discharge in 1958, I had the good fortune to meet the love of my life, Alice, who became my wife one year later. For the following two years, I studied engineering and architecture in Pittsburgh.

In 1960, Alice and I settled in northern Virginia where I had been selected for a position in engineering and architecture. We then began to raise our family. Our son Frank III was born in 1961, our daughter Patsy in 1962. Shortly after, I began once again to enroll in college courses.

Throughout the years after I left my boyhood home, when the green leaves began to turn to red, gold and yellow; when the frost began to coat the window panes and ice began to form at the edges of the streams and ponds; I began to hear the howling of beagles in pursuit in my mind. During those years, when my work and family responsibilities permitted, the legendary horn of the hunter beckoned me home for a few days afield with relatives and old friends.

Upon my return to our home in Virginia, our children were always anxiously awaiting whatever stories of the hunt I had to tell. As they grew older, Frank began to ask when he would be big enough to hunt with me. Patsy seemed to enjoy the stories, but she didn't like guns. She also did not relish the thought of shooting little bunnies, although she seemed to relish the taste of the ones I brought home.

As the years went by and Frank approached the age of ten, I began to think of how rewarding it would be for him to have the opportunity which I had; to grow up with the sport of small game hunting with beagles. I decided then that we should have a beagle of our own.

As it happened, a boyhood friend of mine at the time, Mike Campana, who still resided in the old hometown, owned a female beagle named Molly, of the renowned Pearson Creek bloodline. Molly's grandsire, Pearson Creek

Carson, a name well-known among "beaglers," had sired (fathered) well over one hundred field champions. Mike had purchased Molly from one Ralph McIntire, who happened to be a boyhood friend of my father. Ralph was well-known among beaglers, locally and from afar, as one of the most celebrated and successful dog breeders in the state of Pennsylvania. He specialized in beagles of the Pearson Creek line.

I had hunted with Mike and Molly on a number of occasions, and was much impressed with Molly's routing and circling skills. I was further impressed with her obedience, and the important fact that she promptly returned to her hunter if the rabbit she was chasing should seek refuge in an abandoned groundhog hole.

Having made the decision to once again have a beagle of our own in the family, I contacted Mike and asked if he would consider having Molly bred. Mike replied that he'd rather not. He feared that it might have an adverse effect on her hunting skills. I told him that I'd never heard of that happening, but still he was not convinced.

Then one day, after a few months had passed, Mike contacted me. He had decided to build an addition to his home. He asked if I would design the addition, and what I would like my fee to be. Recognizing a window of opportunity, I replied that I would be pleased to design the addition, and the only payment I'd ask was that he have Molly bred by one of Ralph McIntire's dogs and give me the pick of the litter.

Having discussed my proposal with Ralph, Mike got back to me soon thereafter. He said that Ralph had convinced him that his concern about Molly's skills was unfounded, that he had accepted my offer, and that Molly had been bred.

When I told my son Frank that we were soon to become beagle owners, he was overjoyed. Patsy and Alice were also delighted, but for a different reason than Frank's and my own. There are few things—if anything at all--cuter than beagle puppies, and they make delightful pets. Frank and Patsy decided to name our puppy "Judy," after a beagle that our Uncle Pat once owned, and because I told them that my pick would be a female.

In the meantime, Frank and I set about building a Pennsylvania-style kennel in our back yard and making all the necessary preparations for Judy's arrival. The ensuing few weeks were a time of great anxiety and anticipation for the entire family.

After what seemed like an eternity to our children, Mike called and informed me that the puppies had arrived, and that I should come to Ralph's home without delay and take my pick of the litter. It was essential that I comply, since other prospective buyers were anxious to choose their puppies as well.

On the following weekend Frank and I drove to Reynoldsville. Together, with Mike, we proceeded to Ralph's home where we examined the puppies and chose the one to be named Judy.

At the end of the six week weaning period, Frank and I drove to Reynoldsville again and brought Judy home. Although our entire family was overjoyed with our precious new puppy, little could we have known what a great hunter she was destined to become. Nor could we have foreseen the pleasure, the delight, the companionship, and the bonding she would provide for us throughout the rest of her life.

CHAPTER II
TRAINING JUDY

Judy soon became the joy of our household. Alice, Frank, and Patsy played with her in our fenced-in back yard for hours on end. They threw balls for her to fetch, ran, and played together. They walked her through the neighborhood on a leash. On rainy days, they brought her inside where she romped and played with them.

There is an age-old fallacy, believed to this day by many pseudo-gun dog authorities, that if a dog is made a pet or a playmate, that dog will not become a good hunter. In my own experience, nothing is farther from the truth. However, it's very important that at an early age, whether or not it's been a family pet, the dog must be given exposure to the fields and thickets, and to the scent of game.

9

Our home in Virginia was situated in a moderate-density suburban setting. To our good fortune, when the subdivisions were built, the developers left an area very near our home of perhaps one hundred acres completely intact. That tract of land consisted of several small, open, wooded patches, many briar patches, and places which were overgrown with honeysuckle. That combination of flora provided excellent rabbit cover. Although the tract was relatively small, it was a beagle trainer's dream. It was simply alive with rabbits.

Soon after we brought Judy home, Frank, Patsy, and I began to take her to the wooded area several evenings each week and for a few hours on Saturday or Sunday. We spooked rabbits from their nests, and put Judy on their trails. Although Judy was less than two months old when we began these sessions, she immediately showed interest by sniffing the ground where the rabbit had run.

With each training session, Judy showed improvement by keeping to the scent for greater distances. It wasn't long at all before she began to sound off as the distances became ever greater in length.

Then one evening while Frank was busy with a Boy Scout activity, Patsy and I took Judy to the training ground. Soon after we arrived there, we flushed a rabbit, and I put Judy on its trail. To my pleasant surprise, since she was only about four months old, she stayed with the trail through several difficult briar patches, and circled the rabbit back to where Patsy and I stood. The chase had begun with short yips which readily transformed to the bawl of a beagle in pursuit, which I so badly wanted to hear.

From the beginning, on each occasion when Judy followed a scent, if even for a short distance, we rewarded her with a dog biscuit. But on this special occasion, her first complete chase, we tripled her treat and gave her additional praise.

From that point on, to my great satisfaction, I could see a continual improvement in Judy's routing ability, her skill in circling a rabbit, and her hunting intensity. I could foresee that our little Judy was to become a first-class hunter.

One evening as I prepared to take Judy to the training ground, I asked Alice to come along. She said, "I'd like to, but since Judy looks to me as a playmate,she probably won't want to hunt if I'm there."

I said, "Well, I think it's important that we find out." She agreed then to come along.

In the car on the way to the hunting ground, Judy played with Alice, and appeared to be happy that her playmate had joined us. When we reached the training area, Judy immediately put her nose to the ground in search for the scent of a rabbit. Paying no attention to Alice's presence, she soon routed a rabbit and pursued it in a perfect circle.

We rewarded Judy, returned to the car, and headed for home. During the journey home, Judy played with Alice with apparent pleasure that "Mom" was with us. Alice was pleasantly surprised with the way in which Judy had so quickly transformed from a playful pet to an intense hunter, and had reverted to the behavior of a pet dog at the conclusion of the hunt.

It is important at this point that the origin and history of the beagle breed should be told in summary. The breed originated in the British Isles many centuries ago for the benefit of the sporting nobility. The original purpose was the pursuit of red deer. The breed was refined over the years to develop keen olfactory senses, stamina, obedience, and beauty.

When the beagle was introduced in America, dog handlers continued with the refinement, but worked to adapt the breed to small game hunting rather than the pursuit of deer. Many different bloodlines emerged from this process, resulting in much controversy over which of those were superior.

The urge to take up the scent of a deer does, however, remain hidden in the genes. For this reason many outstanding beagles, including Judy, have been known to normally disregard a fresh deer scent, but when they are taken to a hunting ground where there is a scarcity of small game and they hunt for hours without a chase, they will occasionally chase deer.

When that happens, it often presents a difficult experience for the dog owner. The reason is that a good beagle cannot be called off a chase, and therefore must be headed off and leashed. Since the circle of a white tail deer might consist of a mile or much more, as opposed to the relatively short circle of a cottontail rabbit, considerable leg work by the owner is often required. Moreover, precious time is taken away from the hunt.

It is an injustice, I've always thought, that the beagle is given a low train-ability rating by many canine authorities such as the American Kennel Club. Admittedly, it is somewhat difficult to train a beagle to jump through a hoop, or to parade before a panel of dog show judges without becoming distracted. It should be considered, however, that a thoroughbred beagle's olfactory senses are forty times superior to those of a human being. Therefore, nearly all of the beagle's behavior is dominated by its sense of smell. When attempting to train the beagle to perform the tricks which other breeds are often trained to do, one must bear in mind that this intense sense of smell and centuries old breeding to perform a particular task present distractions.

It is uncommon knowledge outside of the beagler circles that many thoroughbreds are astute game bird hunters as well as fine rabbit dogs. This is particularly true in the case of the aboriginal, ring-necked pheasant. This colorful, pugnacious bird seems to leave a strong scent which, as we will see in later chapters, is attractive to many beagles.

When I became satisfied that Judy had been adequately trained and disciplined for cottontail hunting, I decided that we should try her on pheasants. I happened to be familiar with a State Game Land named "Meadow Grounds" in southern Pennsylvania, where the Pennsylvania Game Commission stocked pheasants.

One Saturday morning, Frank and I loaded Judy in the car, and drove to Meadow Grounds. It was a perfect, early fall morning. The sun shone brightly on the dew-covered high grasses, giving them a crystalline appearance. The wind velocity was minimal.

There was a dual purpose for our outing on that day. First, was my intent to test Judy on pheasant hunting. Next, I wanted to teach Frank the techniques of hunting these birds with a beagle. Since I was training Frank and Judy simultaneously in anticipation of their first hunting experience, this would be an excellent opportunity for both of them to learn together.

Pheasant hunting with a beagle is much different than with a pointer or setter. With those traditional bird dogs, the procedure is to place a bell on the dog's collar, and to move through cover with the dog five to ten yards ahead. When the bell ceases to ring, the hunter knows that there is a concealed bird ahead and that the dog is on point.

With his gun at the ready, the hunter moves forward to flush and shoot the bird.

This is a time-tested procedure which works very well with quail and many other game birds. But in the case of the wily ring-neck, quite often it does not work at all, the reason being that the bird will often not hold for a point, but will take off running on the ground. This results in frustration for the hunter and bewilderment for the dog. I've heard of potentially good bird dogs being nearly ruined by continual experiences of this kind.

On the other hand, if one has the good fortune to hunt with a beagle which is good on pheasants, and if he knows the drill, his game bag will often be filled much sooner than with a bird dog. The method is to proceed, through cover, five to ten paces behind the dog. Watch for the dog's tail to begin to rapidly swing from side to side, then listen for her to begin sounding off, and at the same time increase your pace to maintain reasonable shotgun range. As the dog's speed increases, the shooter's gait must increase as well.

When the bird gets tired of running, he'll stop and prepare to fly. At that point, the dog will crouch and make ready to pounce. The hunter should then prepare to fire. When the dog pounces and the bird becomes airborne, give him a lead and get on him quickly. They're tough birds, and of course the longer the shot, the less the likelihood of a clean kill.

Prior to the trip to Meadow Grounds, I had explained to Frank the procedures and the merits of hunting pheasants with a beagle. While we were en route that morning, I went over them again so they'd be fresh in his mind.

We parked perhaps one hundred yards below a feed plot, where the Game Commission had planted rows of corn with forage turnips on one side, and soy beans on the other. The plot was about two hundred yards long. Most of the corn stalks had been broken down by feeding game, but much corn remained, and the stubble provided excellent cover.

We started in at the lower edge of the corn field. I had told Frank to bring his shotgun along so that he could practice honing in on a flushed bird. The legal hunting season was not in, so he left his ammunition at home. He fell in at the proper distance behind Judy with his gun at high port, just like a pro.

We hadn't gone far until Judy's tail began to wag furiously. Then, she began to sound off with short yelps which changed to howling as she broke into a run.

Without being told, Frank began to run behind her. They continued on a fairly regular course for approximately fifty yards. Then, Judy stopped and crouched. When she pounced, a magnificent cock bird took to the air. Frank threw down on him, and faked a shot as he'd been instructed.

I praised Frank for a job well done. We rewarded Judy with a few treats, and made a fuss over her for her excellent work. We then went about our attempt to hunt up another bird.

We flushed two more pheasants that day, another cock bird, and a hen. In each case, both Frank and Judy performed admirably, much to my satisfaction.

At the close of that perfect day, as the sun began to set beyond the surrounding hills and a slight chill became noticeable in the pleasant breeze, Frank, Judy, and I proceeded to our car and began our two-hour journey home. Like a typical hound, Judy wolfed down the remainder of the treats we had brought with us, after which she curled up between us for a long-awaited nap after a hard day's work.

Frank and I fell into a conversation mainly concerning the practice hunt of that day. We talked about the approaching hunting season, when at long last he'd be old enough to accompany me to the forests and fields. With his inquisitive nature, he had many questions concerning the use of firearms, the handling of dogs, and the hunting rules and regulations.

From the warmth and relaxation of the car and the fatigue from an active day afield, Frank soon joined Judy with a nap that would last until we arrived at home.

For the remainder of the journey I was alone with my thoughts. I thought of how thankful I was to have a fine young son who shared my interests and would soon become my hunting partner. I thought of how blessed I was that a comfortable home, a loving wife, and a beautiful little girl were faithfully waiting at the end of my ride.

As I glanced over at Frank and Judy, I was pleased for having the foresight to obtain Judy in adequate time to have her trained for my son's first hunting season. It was gratifying to know that he would soon experience many exhilarating hunts, as I had as a boy, so many years before.

As my thoughts returned to preparing for the small game season, I decided that there was one remaining test which Judy should be given. Her reaction to gunfire must be tested.

It's a very uncommon occurrence, but I had known of cases when gun dogs were well-trained from the time they were very young and showed much promise, but when they first heard the report of their masters' guns, they cowered and lost the will to continue the chase.

Understandably, this resulted in great frustration and disappointment for the dog owners.

I thought it very unlikely that Judy would display a sign of gun-shyness. She seemed very well adjusted, showed no shyness, and reacted well to the presence of strangers. Nonetheless, we had gone to great lengths to train her, and I wanted to be sure all the bases were covered.

Alice, the kids, and I had planned to visit our families in Pennsylvania on the following weekend. I decided that the wooded areas surrounding my boyhood home would be the perfect place to conduct the test. In the vicinity of our Virginia home, it was unlawful to discharge firearms, which was also the case on state game lands except during the designated hunting seasons. But, in a rural setting such as Reynoldsville, Pennsylvania, we'd be free, within limits, to do as we wished.

On the following Friday evening, we stowed everything we'd need in our car, including Judy, and Frank's shotgun with plenty of ammunition, and headed north. Judy, by this time, associated a ride in the car with an opportunity to chase bunnies. As a result, she was overcome with anxiety, and jumped from the back seat to the front and back again continually until we reached our destination.

On the following morning, Frank, Judy, and I headed for the wood lots accompanied by a life-long friend and neighbor, Friz Harmon. Friz and I had hunted together since my boyhood. He was an accomplished beagle trainer, and I was anxious to hear his evaluation of Judy.

In no time at all Judy picked up a scent, routed the rabbit and went on with the chase. As I instructed, Frank fired his gun into the air several times while the chase was in progress. Not once was Judy's steady bawl interrupted or altered by the sound of gunfire. To my satisfaction, I knew then that whatever concern I had about gun-shyness was completely unfounded. I was exceptionally pleased when Friz remarked about how well Judy routed and circled, and what an extraordinary running voice she had, since Friz, like Ralph McIntire, was considered an authority by the beagler community, and had owned and trained many gun dogs.

There were additional traits and positive habits Judy would come to learn and apply as time went on, such as the important skill of game retrieval. Most of them, however, could only be developed during the hunting seasons when game was brought down in front of her. But, after she passed the gunfire test and we leashed her and headed home, I knew in my heart that she was destined to become an outstanding gun dog and a beloved member of our family. I knew that Frank and I were about to embark on a journey of many years, with countless memorable hunts and rewarding days.

CHAPTER III
THE MAKING OF A HUNTER

At the time we brought Judy home, our son Frank III was nearly eleven years old. In August of the following year, he would reach the age of twelve, and be eligible for his first hunting license.

As I've mentioned, my primary purpose for acquiring a beagle was that my son should be afforded the opportunity, as I had as a youth, to grow up with the extremely rewarding experience of small game hunting with a thoroughbred gun dog.

The more we continued to train Judy, the more appreciative I became of how fortunate we were to have picked such an exceptional dog for Frank to spend his formative hunting years with. In time to come, with so many great adventures afield, I would become increasingly thankful for our good fortune.

In addition to training Judy, there was another enjoyable task at hand. Although I had exposed our son to the use and handling of firearms during several previous years to a great extent, I felt it was important during the months leading up to his first hunting season that I should help him as much as possibleto be fully prepared.

At that time I was First Vice President of a very active rod and gun and conservation club near our home. Frank had already fired on our skeet and trap ranges, but now it was time to intensify his training and familiarization with emphasis on safety precautions.

At our skeet and trap range he became competent with light gauge shotguns under the tutelage of our range officer and instructor, my good old friend Phil Godfrey.

Phil, a World War II Marine veteran, was an excellent instructor and superb shooter. He had won several awards for breaking one thousand clay birds without a miss. He was a no-nonsense man who demanded undivided attention and perfection from his students.

Frank required rifle marksmanship training as well as with the shotguns, since I planned to take him deer hunting after the small game season expired. Under my own instruction, he became an adept marksman at our rifle range.

I've always been a firm believer in the merits of providing a beginning hunter with a single shot piece. First of all, the beginner comes to understand the importance of marksmanship when the first and only shot must count. All too frequently, those who begin with repeating arms put too little emphasis on the first shot, knowing that they have a second or third round to fall back on.

For these reasons and for posterity, when Frank became ten years old I gave my first shotgun, the little Stevens .410 single shot, to him.

I shall always remember the day when I handed the little shotgun to him and told him it was his own. He was overcome with pride and delight. He treasured that gun, not so much for what it was, but because it had been his dad's first gun many years earlier. Soon, he would proudly carry it on many successful hunts.

Frank had been firing the .410 for a year or two and had become proficient with its use and handling. But now that it was his own he took special pride in his shooting ability and in the care and cleaning of his gun.

On several of our trips to the training grounds with Judy, I had him carry his gun, unloaded of course, to familiarize him with the techniques of hunting rabbits with a dog.

On one occasion, which I described in the previous chapter, he carried his gun when we tested Judy on hunting ring-necked pheasants. As I pointed out, both he and Judy performed to my great satisfaction.

In the late summer and early fall of each year prior to the hunting seasons, our sportsman's club held a turkey shoot each Friday evening. The shoots were open to the public for a fee, and the proceeds were used for maintenance and improvements to our buildings and grounds.

The shooting sessions were conducted as follows:

Six shooters stood side by side at the firing line, each facing a separate paper target which had been placed on a post fifty feet down range. Beginning on the left, the range officer handed the first shooter a live shotgun round. The shooter would then fire at his target, on which his assigned number was printed. The range officer would then move to shooter number two and so on down the line until each shooter had fired.

The targets were then collected and judged to determine the winner. The winner was determined by the shot (BB) hole nearest to dead center of the target.

Each year we reserved a Saturday evening for youth from ten to sixteen years of age. The shoot was a part of our outdoor sports training program for young people.

Frank, of course, was anxious to test his skill at the shoot with his .410.

On the evening of the shoot, just before he and I departed for the club, his mom told him, "Now you be sure to bring a turkey home. It's getting close to Thanksgiving."

"I will, Mom," he said with confidence.

As the shooters lined up Frank stepped into position like a veteran. And when the targets were judged, lo and behold, he was the winner. "Boy," he said, beaming with pride, "I can't wait to tell Mom."

When we arrived home that evening, I had hardly stopped the car when he jumped out, frozen turkey in hand, and hastened to present it to his mom. It was a moment of great pride and satisfaction for the entire family. We all gave him many words of praise.

As we partook in the Thanksgiving festivities that fell in the company of my aunt and uncle, Frank was the "man of the hour" for having provided the traditional turkey.

As the opening day of the Pennsylvania small game season drew near, I became satisfied that Frank was much better prepared than the average beginning hunter. He was well-versed in the safe handling and care of firearms. He had developed the stamina and physical endurance for a long, hard day's hunt. He had become adept at gun dog handling and care, and the field procedures of hunting small game with a dog. And to my great satisfaction, a lasting bond had begun to develop between him and our lovable dog, Judy.

CHAPTER IV
THE FIRST HUNT

The day we had long awaited finally arrived. It was the Saturday nearest November first, the traditional opening day of the Pennsylvania small game season.

I awakened Frank long before daylight, and we began to prepare for the drive to the hunting ground. Great care was taken to be sure we loaded all the essentials for our day's hunt.

As we savored the logger's breakfast which Alice had prepared, Judy began to howl excitedly from the confines of her kennel to the point where we brought her into the house lest she awaken the neighbors. In time to come, we would receive anonymous letters and phone calls from unhappy neighbors whose sleep was interrupted by

Judy's unwelcome serenade in the early morning hours. To this day, I've been unable to figure out how she differentiated between a hunting day and any other day. We routinely awakened early, had breakfast together, then hurried off to work and school every day with the exception of Saturday and Sunday. But somehow, she always knew when it was a day to hunt.

We soon headed north to our destination. We'd planned to hunt that day on a sprawling two-thousand acre farm which straddled the Mason-Dixon line at the boundary between Pennsylvania and Maryland. The farm, owned by our old friends Sam and Jean McNabb, was steeped in history. Jean had once shown me the original deed which certified that it had been purchased soon after the American Revolution by Sam's ancestor. It was bought from Steven Penn, a relative of William Penn, in pounds sterling. It was said that several Civil War skirmishes were fought there just before the Union and Confederate forces engaged at Gettysburg, ten miles to the north.

The McNabb farm was also rich in American Indian lore. On several occasions, Sam had shown me the many artifacts he had found in the course of his life.

The farm consisted of huge grain fields, pastures studded with briar patches, and many dense cedar thickets. That combination presented excellent feed and cover, and game abounded there. I had enjoyed many successful hunts there in previous years.

After a one-and-a-half hour drive, we reached our destination in plenty of time to walk to the area which I had decided upon to begin our hunt, with Judy straining impatiently at her leash. At 8:00 AM, the legal starting time on opening day, we loaded our guns, released Judy, and got into position to comb the thickets.

As we began to move in, Frank and I were perhaps twenty yards apart with Judy between us and five to ten yards forward. I was certain that there were rabbits here, for Judy almost immediately began working from side to side with her nose to the ground, sniffing loudly.

We hadn't gone far until Judy's tail began to wag furiously. Suddenly, the trail became hot, and she started her familiar yip which soon transformed to a howl.

I motioned for Frank to stay put as Judy proceeded into heavier cover. Her howling increased at shorter intervals, and I knew she'd routed the rabbit at the far edge of the cover.

As Judy continued her pursuit downhill into a small, brush-covered valley, I could tell the rabbit was beginning to circle to the left. I approached Frank and helped him select a good vantage point on high ground, in case the rabbit would make a complete circle in an attempt to return to its safe haven, as they often do. I selected a position for myself from where I could clearly see Frank and perhaps catch a glimpse of the rabbit as Judy continued to push in a circle back toward the cover.

As Judy's sounding off began to get closer, I knew that the rabbit could show up at any moment, provided it didn't make an unexpected turn. I motioned to Frank where I thought the rabbit would approach, and he focused in that direction.

Suddenly, I caught a glimpse of the rabbit as it broke across a narrow opening in the direction of the cover. I motioned again to Frank, and pointed to where I'd seen the rabbit.

A few moments later, Frank raised his gun, followed through, and fired. He reloaded and hurried to the spot where the rabbit had crossed.

I approached Frank and asked, "Did you get him?"

"No," he replied with a look of disappointment. "I missed and he got away."

"Don't be too sure yet," I said. "Let's stand back and let Judy finish the chase."

Frank showed me where the rabbit had gone into the cover and with optimism, I noticed a few tufts of rabbit hair. We backed off then to avoid distracting Judy.

Judy approached and entered the thicket where the rabbit had been when Frank fired. Then suddenly, her howling ceased.

A few moments later, she came marching proudly from the thicket with her head and tail lifted high, and with Frank's rabbit clenched between her teeth. "You see," I said. "Never give up until the chase is over. Remember the old saying, 'The show's not over 'till the fat lady sings.'"

Judy laid the rabbit at our feet and looked up as if to ask, "How did I do?" Frank reached down and hugged her, and gave her a biscuit.

This was a time of great satisfaction and pride for all of us. Frank was overjoyed, but no more than I was. My son had shot his first rabbit, and Judy had made her first retrieval.

I congratulated Frank, praised Judy, and took some photos with the little Minolta which I carried in my pocket. Then, I gave Frank a lesson in field dressing a rabbit.

After removing the gall bladder, I gave Judy the heart and liver. This is a customary ritual among Pennsylvania beaglers which is said to make the dog a more intense hunter. I don't know how much truth there is to that, but Judy enjoyed those morsels nonetheless.

We stowed Frank's rabbit in his game pocket and I asked Frank if he was ready to find another one.

"You bet I am, Dad," he replied. So, we headed off in the direction of more dense cover adjacent to a harvested grain field.

As we combed the thickets, Judy soon picked up another scent. This time the rabbit ranged farther out ahead than usual. When Judy's voice told us he was swinging to the right, Frank and I moved ahead somewhat since I anticipated that the circle would be completed farther out than where we were positioned.

As the rabbit began to circle, Judy's howl suddenly ceased. We waited ten to fifteen minutes before I began to call her to mark our position. Presently, she came running back to us.

"What happened, Dad?" Frank asked. "Why did she quit the chase?"

"The rabbit holed up," I said. And although we did not get an opportunity for a shot, I was greatly pleased. I explained to Frank that Judy had just displayed another good quality. When she'd discovered that the rabbit had holed she came back to us, enabling us to resume our hunt. Many dogs will remain there, digging at the hole or drifting off in that vicinity searching for another scent. The hunters then lose valuable time searching for their dogs.

To that I added, "On a farm like this one, where there's an abundance of groundhogs and many abandoned holes, what you've just seen happen could well be a common occurrence."

Plenty of time remained for another chase before lunch. We decided to work our way toward the farmhouse through an area of dense briar patches. I advised Frank that if a rabbit should be routed here, he should quickly make his way to the edge of the briar patch where he'd have a better opportunity for a shot.

As we struggled through the briars, I soon saw a rabbit scoot out in front of me. Not wanting to deny Judy a chase, I did not shoot. I advanced to the spot where I'd seen the rabbit and called Judy to me. I put my finger to the ground and said, "There goes a bunny."

From that point on throughout her life, when a hunting partner or I would flush a rabbit or a pheasant, I needed only to shout the word "bunny," or say "there he goes," and Judy would come running to begin the chase. I had to avoid those words in her presence unless there was, in fact, game to be pursued.

Immediately Judy began to sound off on the chase. I looked in Frank's direction and saw that he had situated himself on a large rock at the edge of the patch to my left. I gave him the okay sign as I hastened to the opposite side of the patch.

Judy stuck to the chase in the difficult cover exceptionally well, but she was unable to get the rabbit to leave the protective briars. Instead, the chase consisted of several short circles within the patch.

From my vantage point, I finally caught a long enough glimpse of the rabbit to crank off a shot. With the report of my 12 gauge, the rabbit tumbled, then lay still.

I waited there until Judy completed the chase. She picked the rabbit up, shook him several times, carried him from the briars, and laid him at my feet.

Frank came over, we dressed the rabbit, and put him in my game pocket. Frank said, "Gosh, Dad, this has been a really great morning."

"It certainly has, old buddy," I replied. "It doesn't get much better than this. It's almost noon. I'm beginning to get a little hungry. How about you?"

As I suspected, he agreed that he was. So, we headed off in the direction of the farmhouse.

We unloaded our guns, secured our gear, praised Judy for an admirable morning's work, and gave her food and water. She then curled up on the car seat for a nap.

Frank grabbed our lunch bucket which his mom had stuffed with sandwiches made with her homemade bread. We proceeded to the farmhouse where we had lunch in the good company of Jean and Sam. Our lunch was augmented with a bowl of hot soup which Jean had prepared.

Frank proudly told Sam and Jean his rabbit story in detail. They congratulated him and gave him much praise and encouragement. After swapping a few good hunting stories with Sam and thanking Jean for her hospitality, I said to Frank, "It's time we get out there and scare up some more game, don't you think?"

He agreed enthusiastically and we grabbed our hats. As we departed Sam said to Frank, "When you shoot, don't you miss, or I'll have to cut off your shirt-tail." This is another age-old custom among Pennsylvania hunters which I had relayed to Frank long before.

Refreshed from her nap and anxious to begin the afternoon hunt, Judy began to work back and forth as soon as we made it to the thickets. We loaded our guns and made ready for our afternoon hunt.

We bagged two more rabbits on that day. Frank missed one which I shot a few minutes later as Judy pushed him to within my range. Frank asked, "Will Sam really cut off my shirt-tail?"

I laughed and said, "If you don't have a good excuse he just might," I added, "Misses happen to the best of us. They're part of the sport, and I've experienced plenty of them myself. Maybe we'll just avoid telling Sam unless he asks."

Frank grinned in agreement as we field-dressed the rabbit. We rewarded Judy and went on with the hunt.

Soon after, Frank made a perfect shot as Judy pushed a rabbit from a thick stand of scrub cedar interspersed with thorn apple. He wanted to dress the rabbit by himself, and he followed the procedure which he'd observed quite well.

Toward evening as we began to work our way back to the farmhouse and passed through the edge of a corn stubble field, Judy worked up a handsome cock pheasant. The bird went up forward of Frank and he followed through and fired, but I suspect the bird was a little far out for the range of his little .410. When the bird veered slightly in my direction, I triggered my full choke barrel and brought him to the ground with a thud. Judy quickly pounced on him and brought him to me.

By the time we reached the farmhouse, dusk was beginning to fall and the temperature had dropped considerably. The gathering dark clouds suggested that snow squalls were imminent.

We stopped at the farmhouse, quickly skinned a couple of rabbits, and gave them to Sam and Jean. We thanked them for the privilege of hunting there, said our goodbyes, and headed for home.

Judy curled up between us again for a well-deserved long snooze after a hard and successful day's work. Frank and I began to talk over the day's hunt, recapping each chase. Presently Frank said, "Gosh, Dad, I really love to hunt. How soon can we do this again?"

"We'll go at it every chance we get until the end of the season," I said, "if that's what you'd like to do."

He confirmed as I'd hoped, that he'd like that more than anything else. He soon drifted off to sleep.

31

As I continued the drive home, in my thoughts I recalled each event of the day, receiving great satisfaction from each of them. I was most pleased that my son had shot his first game animal, that he had done so well in terms of marksmanship and safety measures, and that he was to become an intense hunter.

I knew that he'd have delightful tales to tell his mom and little sister when we arrived home and had shared the chores of gun cleaning and preparing our game for the freezer. I was sure that he'd revel in telling his story of this day's great success to his friends in the neighborhood and at school. I knew also that his account would be embellished with the greatness of our extraordinary gun dog and companion, Judy.

CHAPTER V
THE OLD STONE FENCE

A few years before Frank was old enough to hunt I became acquainted with the Simmons family, who lived in a mobile home on several acres of ground near the borough of Everett, Pennsylvania. The Simmons' home was surrounded by a farm of several hundred acres, owned by an elderly gentleman, Mr. Morgan.

Mr. Simmons, nicknamed "Chub," had obtained permission from Mr. Morgan for me to hunt the farm. So, one Friday evening I said to Frank, "Let's try the Morgan farm tomorrow. I've never hunted there, but there's bound to be plenty of game feed and it will be good to check out some different territory."

With Frank in agreement, we set out before daylight the next morning with Judy between us, for a new adventure.

After a drive of a little more than two hours, we arrived at our destination just as the sun came up from behind the surrounding hills. The night before had been clear, cold, and dry. Experience had taught me that game animals do not move and feed on that kind of night as readily as they do on a night that is overcast, and the ground is moist and frost-free. I anticipated that Judy would need to work harder to find scent that morning, putting her to yet another test.

On that farm, a greater percentage of the acreage consisted of grain fields than on the much larger McNabb farm. The few wooded patches and thickets were confined to areas not conducive to the growing of crops. They did, however, offer inviting sanctuaries for the game which feasted on Mr. Morgan's nearby grain fields.

We parked near the Simmons' home, crossed the road, and headed out with Judy in the lead toward some wooded areas which I could see far in the distance.

The foot-high grass in the field we were crossing was covered with a heavy frost, and the high stalks in an adjacent uncut cornfield glistened in the rising sun. The air was still, without even a hint of a breeze.

Experience reminded me that rabbits and birds will sit very tight on a morning like this, and we'd need to work the cover very thoroughly in order to flush them. I explained this to Frank as we continued toward the thickets. I added that in the afternoon, when the sun had melted the frost, the game would likely return to the grain fields to feed and we should hunt there then.

As we approached the thickets I knew there were cold trails in the high grass from the way that Judy worked. Cold trailing is typical of a good dog on a frosty morning.

When we reached the thicket, we found that it consisted of widely-interspersed large red oaks, many thorn apples, and very dense briars. This combination offers some of the best game cover, but is very difficult for the hunter or the dog to penetrate.

Frank and I spread out to a distance of twenty yards. I told him that when a chase begins he should hasten to a spot where a reasonably good view would be possible. I reminded him that the game would be sitting tight, and although it would be difficult, we'd need to pound the cover very thoroughly. I also mentioned that I predicted a rabbit would run short circles in order to remain in the protective cover. I added that there were probably many groundhog holes here and not to be surprised if we should have a few hole-ups, particularly on a frosty morning.

Without any hesitation Judy plunged into the thick, jagged briars. In our attempt to follow her, we tried to stomp every conceivable place where we thought a rabbit might be hiding.

Without the benefit of a good routing dog, it's difficult to get a shot off in this kind of cover. Many times a rabbit will scoot out ahead of the hunter without being seen. Also, when the hunter is up to his neck in thorny briars, it's often impossible for him to get his gun in position in time to fire.

In about ten minutes, I began to hear Judy yip from perhaps twenty yards ahead. When the yip changed to her familiar bawl, I called to Frank and said, "There's a rabbit out now, try to get to a good position and be perfectly still. He'll be close before you see him and he'll spook easily."

By Judy's voice I could tell that the rabbit was hopping around in short circles at a relatively short distance ahead of her, exactly as I'd suspected considering the conditions.

When perhaps twenty minutes had drifted by with Judy continually sounding off, I heard the report of Frank's .410. I could not see him well through the brush, but I heard the breach of his gun close as he reloaded.

I remained in position and continued to strain my eyes into the thicket, hoping for a glimpse of an approaching rabbit. Judy had continued to howl without interruption long after Frank had fired, so I knew the rabbit was still up and running.

A short distance to my left stood the remains of an old stone fence. The fence, which had undoubtedly been built by settlers many years earlier, had fallen down in many places. The parts which remained were about one and one half feet tall, and partly overgrown with weeds.

Suddenly, from the corner of my eye, I saw the rabbit struggling along toward me on top of the stone fence. I could readily tell from the rabbit's movement that Frank had scored a hit which had slowed its pace, but had obviously not been fatal.

As I raised my double barrel and made ready to fire, the rabbit all of a sudden vanished from site. As I waited for Judy to complete her chase, a reasonably good idea of what had happened occurred to me. In all likelihood, the rabbit had concealed itself beneath one of the larger stones in the wall.

Presently, Judy came stumbling along, trying to stay atop the broken-down wall. She completed the chase at the large stone where I'd last seen the rabbit.

Judy began to scratch at the stone and howl as I had predicted. I summoned Frank, and he began to make his way through the thorns toward my position.

As Frank continued to approach, Judy suddenly seemed to lose interest in the rabbit, put her nose to the air, and began to drift off toward the edge of the thicket some twenty yards away. Surprised at her behavior, I called, "Judy, come back here and find the bunny."

When she paid no attention I went after her, picked her up, and carried her back to the stone. Immediately she drifted away as she had before toward the edge of the thicket, where it gave way to an open area covered with goldenrod and swale grass.

When Judy reached the open area her tail began to wag furiously, and she began to yip. At that point I thought, "What a fool I am." As a seasoned hunter and with my confidence in Judy, I should have known what was happening.

I yelled to Frank, "Hurry and come out here! She's working a pheasant up." Frank unfortunately was bogged down in the briars and was unable to get out of them quickly enough.

Judy's voice in the meantime had changed from a yip to a bawl as she pursued the pheasant through the cover. In my attempt to keep up with her, I began to run through the impeding high weeds. The bird ran no more than thirty yards until Judy got too close for his comfort and, with a scolding cackle, he flushed.

I threw down on the multi-colored, majestic cock bird for a straight-away shot, triggered my modified barrel, and brought him down with a direct hit.

As Frank made his way out into the field, Judy pounced on the bird and brought him to me. Immediately, without even waiting for her treat, she began to run back in the direction of the rock.

As I began to run after Judy, Frank said "Dad, I'm sure I hit that rabbit. I found a handful of hair where he was when I shot."

I said, "You hit him, alright, Buddy. I've a pretty good idea where he is. Let's go."

As quickly as we could, we made our way back to the stone fence where Judy was already whining and scratching at the big stone. I said to Frank, "You hold onto her while I see if I can move the rock."

When Frank took Judy's collar and pulled her back, she began to howl and strain at her collar. I bent down and began to move the rock.

When I succeeded in removing the rock from the wall, a rather large cavity was revealed. At the floor of the cavity lay Frank's rabbit.

I said, "Now let her go." The moment she became free she leaped into the cavity and came out with the lifeless animal clenched in her teeth.

She shook the rabbit a few times, then laid it at our feet. Frank gave her a hug, then whipped out his treat bag and rewarded her.

As we field dressed the rabbit I said to Frank, "We have a truly exceptional gun dog here, Buddy. In all the years I've hunted, never before have I seen a performance like that. For her to wind a bird at that distance, and go for him knowing that her rabbit would run no farther, then to come back to him when the bird was down without being urged is a rare performance, especially in her first year afield."

We stowed the bird and rabbit in our game bags and continued to hunt the thicket. After a short time Frank said "There's surely another rabbit in all this cover."

38

"You can pretty well bet there is," I said. And, sure enough, within a few minutes Judy began to sound off again.

Like the one before, this rabbit began to run short circles within the thick patch. Finally, I dumped him as he ventured near the edge.

By the time we dressed and stowed that rabbit it was nearly noon. The sun had burned off the heavy morning frost, and the temperature had risen by at least twenty degrees.

We agreed to pack it in for the morning, have some lunch, and shed some clothing. We'd give Judy a rest and then hit it again in the afternoon.

I'd predicted and mentioned again to Frank that the game would likely move into the feeding areas toward evening, and I was therefore optimistic about our afternoon hunt. With that in mind, we made our way toward the Simmons' home.

We shed our heavy hunting coats and stowed our game in our cooler. We leashed Judy to a tree in the shade, and gave her treats and water. We then had lunch in the company of Chub, Mrs. Simmons, and their son and daughter at a picnic table in their back yard. Over lunch, our friends listened attentively as Frank told the story of our morning hunt.

Chub, who had been an avid hunter in his younger days, was fascinated with the incident at the stone fence. "Never heard of a dog performing like that," he said.

Chub, who was at that time past the age of sixty, went on to say he knew exactly where that old stone fence was. It had been there ever since he could remember, and when he was a boy the deteriorated remains of a settler's cabin stood near it.

Soon I said to Frank, "Well, let's put on our light-weight vests and get back out there." When we stood, Judy knew it was time to hunt again, and began to jump up and down, straining at her leash in eagerness.

We did quite well on that magnificent autumn day. We each bagged another rabbit, and I managed to bring down another cock bird after Judy had worked up two hens. Judy had only one hole-up that entire day.

On our journey home while Judy slept between us, in conversation we relived our successful day's hunt. We agreed on our good fortune for having such an exceptional gun dog as Judy. And we both knew in our hearts that we'd always remember our experience at the old stone fence.

CHAPTER VI
FRANK'S FIRST PHEASANT

In August of the following year, we celebrated Frank's thirteenth birthday. Already we were beginning to talk about the fall and the ensuing small game season.

Frank had grown considerably taller over the past year and had become a pretty husky lad with broad shoulders. He was a veteran hunter now, having been successfully broken in the previous year.

It occurred to me that perhaps it was time for him to graduate to a larger gauge gun. This would give him an edge over his little .410, particularly with ring-necked pheasants.

As a rule, Frank and I spent some time on weekends at the ranges of our sportsman's club. I thought the skeet and trap ranges there would be an excellent setting for him to try out the bigger guns. I'd have him begin with a 20 gauge and see how well he did. Then, if he wished, we'd try him out with a 16 gauge. If he was comfortable with the increased recoil and if he so desired, perhaps we'd even go to a 12 gauge.

At the first opportunity, we went to the trap range where Frank shot several rounds of birds under further instruction from my great friend Phil Godfrey.

After that first session, during which he did quite well, Frank said," Dad, I notice little if any difference between my .410 and the 20 gauge. Could I try something bigger?"

"Certainly," I replied. "But bear in mind, as the gauge increases so does the recoil and the weight."

"I know," he said. "But so does my chance with a pheasant."

I said, "While that may be true up to a point, observation and experience have taught me that a man is usually more successful with a small gun with which he's comfortable than a big gun with which he's not. Keep that in mind on our next trip to the range."

The following weekend we returned to the range with four guns. We brought a 16 gauge side by side double, a 12 gauge side by side, a 12 gauge slide (pump) action, and a 12 gauge single shot.

Frank fired a few rounds from each gun that afternoon and did reasonably well with all of them. He handled the 12 gauge single best of all.

When I asked about the recoil, I was greatly pleased with his reply. "I was concentrating on hitting the clay bird and the kick didn't bother me at all. I didn't even think about it."

I asked, " Well, do you think you'd like to hunt with one of the bigger guns this year, and if so, which of the four are you most comfortable with?"

"I like the 12 gauge single the best," he replied. "For one thing, it's much lighter in weight than the others. And then I like the breach-loading action, which is just like my .410. It's easier to load than the other actions even though you don't have a back-up shot."

I asked, "Are you sure you wouldn't rather hunt with one of the doubles? The break-open breech-loading action is the same as the single."

"No, Dad," he said. "They're too heavy. I'm used to a single barrel, and I like the idea of focusing on the game the way you taught me, and making the first shot count. Maybe later on I'll want to switch to one of the others, but for this season I'd like to carry the 12 single."

I said, "Okay, Partner. From now until the season begins, let's bring it to the range as often as we can. You'll be a crack shot with it by the time the season begins."

So, until opening day grew near, Frank shot a round (25 shots) of clay birds nearly every weekend. Compliments from my old friend Phil Godfrey, a World War II Marine Sergeant, were hard-earned. So, I was pleased when he praised Frank and told me that the boy did well. Phil's nickname for Frank incidentally was "Buckshot," which Frank seemed to like quite well.

At one point, Frank asked, "Dad, why do you always use a double barrel when you'd have more back-up shots with a pump gun?"

"Good question," I said. "The main reason is, with a double, you have the option of two different chokes. There are 3 standard chokes, by the way. There's the cylinder bore, which is commonly used by quail hunters and for shooting other small game birds. The modified choke is commonly used for a little larger upland game, such as rabbits and pheasants. Then there's the full choke, which holds the shot pattern together at a longer range. The full choke is the favorite of water fowlers and turkey hunters. Over the years, I've found that the most advantageous barrels for the hunting we normally do is the modified and full choke combination. Normally, I fire the modified barrel first. But, there have been many occasions when a pheasant or a rabbit has been flushed far out ahead, and I've been glad to have the capability to switch to the full choke barrel. I've found this to be more to my advantage than the alternative option of a third shot. Furthermore, I've always said that if I can't score with two shots, I don't deserve the game anyway."

Frank said, "That makes a lot of sense, Dad. I'm glad I asked. I'll probably switch to a double later on, but this year I think I'd still like to use that single."

In the meantime, we continued religiously to take Judy to our training ground several times each week. Her routing and circling skills continued to improve as time went on, and we looked forward to a productive shooting season.

On a number of occasions, my old friend and neighbor Fred Wenzel, who was another lifelong gun dog enthusiast, accompanied us. Fred marveled at Judy's performance and told me how he'd love to have a dog just like her. "In my experience," I said, "unfortunately, there aren't many of those available."

On one unusually warm evening, Frank, Fred, and I were walking up a grade at the training ground with Judy a few yards ahead. Judy suddenly stopped, moved her nose up and down, looked back at us, then walked around to the right of the place where she had stopped. Keeping her eyes on that spot, she continued her half

44

circle until she soon picked up her original course and proceeded up the hill.

"I'll bet there's a snake there," I said. With my walking stick, I began to poke at the spot.

Suddenly, a squadron of ground yellow jackets converged upon me from their grass-covered hole. In seconds they were all over me, stinging me multiple times. I ran back from the hole swatting furiously. When my attackers had either been swatted or had returned to their hole, I noticed Judy looking back at me. I could have sworn I saw a look of amusement in her big brown eyes.

Fred said to me, "It looks like that dog has more smarts than you do, Frank." I had to admit that, at least in this case, he was absolutely right.

As the air began to cool, the deciduous trees began to show a trace of color, and the scents of autumn began to fill the air, the hunting urge began to stir within my son and me. We talked about the coming season and the places we planned to hunt. I praised Frank for his improvement in shooting and firearms-handling skills. Judy would go into her second season now, and we looked forward to many exciting chases and new adventures.

As the opening day drew near, we checked out our ammunition supply and made certain that all of our gear was in good shape. We planned to begin the season at the McNabb farm, so I phoned Sam to let him know we'd be there at daybreak on opening day.

On the morning we'd so anxiously awaited, Judy began her usual bawl as soon as we turned on the kitchen lights. Frank brought her in where she played with Alice until we were ready to leave. At one point she wakened Patsy, who sleepily came to see us off and wish us luck.

We arrived at the McNabb farm at daybreak as we'd planned. The sky was overcast and there was a dampness in the still air, suggesting that rain showers could be on the way. I had listened to the weather report before we left home and no heavy precipitation was in the forecast.

While we walked to the area where we'd planned to begin our hunt, I told Frank that I was pleased with my outlook for the day. "Scent hangs long and heavy on a day like this," I said. "It should be a productive day."

We turned Judy loose at the edge of a sprawling pasture which was studded here and there with dense briar patches. Immediately, she began to work steadily from one patch to the other. Frank and I spread out and started to stomp the cover as best we could.

Before long I heard Frank call, "Here, Judy," followed by, "there he goes."

I saw Judy run toward Frank and then heard her bawl as she took up the chase. As he got into position, Frank called to me that when he'd started into the patch, the rabbit had busted out the opposite side. After a long chase, the rabbit circled toward Frank. As I watched, Frank got him broad side with a direct hit.

Judy ran three more rabbits that morning. Frank shot another one. I missed one as I saw him running through one of the briar patches. That one found an old groundhog hole to which he was probably headed and vanished from sight. A short time later, I put one down with a nearly straight-away shot.

Just before we knocked off for lunch, Judy worked up a pheasant. I anxiously waited for Frank to get off a shot with his 12 gauge, but to our disappointment, the bird was a hen which was protected by law.

Over lunch I mentioned to Sam that I'd missed a rabbit. Sam said, "Jean, where's your scissors?"

"I don't know," she said. "I'll have to look for them."

I said to Frank, "Come on, we'd better get out there before Jean finds her scissors. This is a new Woolrich shirt I have on."

Judy had three chases early that afternoon. I shot the first two rabbits. The third one ran two complete circles unseen and then holed up.

Toward evening, we started into a field which Sam had planted with sweet corn. The corn ears had been harvested months before, and most of the stalks were broken down. Sweet corn stalks are not nearly so tall as those of field corn, so I knew that those still standing would not hamper our visibility.

We hadn't gone far when Judy's tail began to quickly whip from side to side. In a few moments, she began to yip and then bawl as she broke into a run.

I called to Frank, "She's on a bird. Now keep up with her."

We ran behind Judy to the far end of the field which was a distance of perhaps sixty yards. At that point, the cornfield abutted a field of knee high swale grass. As Judy continued into the grass, Frank said, "Dad, are you sure that's a bird? It seems to have run an awful long way."

I said, "There's no doubt in my mind it's a bird. You'll eventually see them run much farther than that. Now keep up with her and don't drop your guard."

About twenty-five yards into the swale, Judy abruptly stopped and crouched. I said, "Watch it, Frank." A moment later, up went a scolding, cackling cock pheasant. This was the moment I had been waiting for.

As the bird reached his leveling off point, Frank fired. The bird folded in a cloud of feathers with Frank's direct hit and dropped to the ground.

Judy immediately picked up the bird, shook him a few times, and laid him at Frank's feet. "Well done, son," I said, as Frank reached down for his first pheasant and held it aloft.

We both laughed, rewarded Judy, and stood there and talked over this great event for a long time. I knew that I was just as excited about it, if not more so, than Frank was.

Finally I said, "Well, it's starting to get late. We'd better begin to work our way toward the farmhouse."

By the time we reached the car, a light rain had begun to fall. We dried Judy with an old towel which we kept in the car for that purpose, and once she was dry, she curled up on her usual spot for her well-earned nap.

Frank summarized the story of his first pheasant to Sam, Who patted Frank on the back, shook his hand, and said, "Good work, boy, congratulations."

We gave Sam a couple rabbits, and thanked him and Jean again for their hospitality and for a great day's hunt on their farm. We said goodbye and that we hoped to see them again soon. Then, we climbed into the car where Judy was already asleep and headed for home.

On our drive home, we critiqued our day's adventure as we usually did. . Frank asked, "Dad, how could you be so sure that Judy was running a bird instead of a rabbit?"

"Good question," I said. "You've probably noticed that the trail of a rabbit is usually somewhat erratic. A pheasant, on the other hand, will usually run in a relatively straight line. In addition to that, with many dogs including Judy, their tone of voice is somewhat different when they're trailing a bird."

Frank said, "I had no idea a pheasant would run that far instead of flying away."

Laughing I responded, "In time, I'm sure you'll see them run much farther than that. I've seen them nearly make a complete circle. I've also seen them take refuge in abandoned groundhog holes. It's happened many times that they've entered a hole, tried to spread their wings, and found themselves trapped. The result, of course, is that the bird dies, and the hole becomes its grave. There have been occasions I've heard, when farmers in the process of their spring plowing, and have uncovered their remains where they had entered holes to escape predators, or perhaps to take refuge from winter storms."

"Wouldn't you think they'd know better than to do that?" Frank asked.

"Well," I said, "let's remember that the ring-necked pheasant is not native to America. It's an oriental bird which was introduced and stocked here a century or more ago for the benefit of the wealthy sporting class on privately-owned shooting preserves. They're still hunted on many preserves to this day. Over the years, however, many of the birds escaped and proliferated in the wild to the good fortune of hunters like you and me. I don't know this for a fact, but perhaps in the ring-neck's native range there are no rodents like groundhogs, and they have not yet evolved to the point where instinct tells them not to enter the holes."

"Anyway, Dad," Frank said, "I'm sure glad somebody brought them here."

"So am I, Buddy," I said. "So am I."

In a few moments, I glanced over and saw that Frank had drifted off to sleep.

Immersed in my own thoughts, I recalled with gratitude the events of another great day afield in the company of my son and Judy. I knew that Frank would again have many stories to tell. On hunts yet to come, he

would bring down many more pheasants. But, I knew
that the one we would always remember most was his
first pheasant flushed on that day by our great gun dog,
Judy.

CHAPTER VII
THE HIDDEN RABBIT

My good friend and neighbor, Fred Wenzel, was a native and life-long resident of Northern Virginia. As a boy, he and his father had hunted in the area surrounding our home, which had been mostly farmland at that time.

As the farmers of Fairfax County began to sell their properties to developers; apartment buildings, single family homes, and business establishments began to take shape and replace the open spaces. The local outdoorsmen were then obliged to look to the West for alternative hunting grounds. Many of them sought the acquaintance of farm owners in the adjacent counties of Loudoun and Prince William.

51

Some years before I came to know Fred, he had become acquainted with the owners of several large farms in rural bordering counties. He had obtained permission to hunt on those farms, and had returned there each fall.

The conditions in that part of Virginia lend well to small game hunting. The winters are not normally severe, and the lush farm fields and areas of dense cover are attractive to the game. Also, hunting pressure is not so intense as it is in many localities. With the combination of all these factors, an abundance of game is usually available for a successful day's hunt.

In his early days, Fred and his father had run beagles. However, not wanting to induce hostility among some of our neighbors as he knew I had, he did not own any beagles at that time. However, he did hunt frequently without the benefit of a dog and occasionally with friends who owned dogs.

One crisp fall evening, Fred happened to see me out raking leaves in front of our house. He walked over, and we began a conversation which soon drifted to rabbit hunting.

After a few stories, Fred began to describe one particular farm in nearby Loudoun County. He hadn't visited the farm that year, but he said in previous years he had bounced a good number of rabbits there. He said he'd made tentative plans to go there on the coming weekend. Prior to hunting there, he always touched base with the owner. He hadn't done that yet, but he'd planned to call that evening.

"Do you think you'd like to come along?" he asked. "I know we'd find rabbits, and I'd love to see Judy hunt."

"I'd be delighted," I said. "But, when you talk with the owner, be sure to ask if it's all right if there are three hunters and a dog this time."

Shortly after, Fred went home and called the owner who lived in the Borough of Leesburg. The owner's farm consisted of about two hundred acres, and was located just a few miles west of the city limits. The owner ran a small herd of beef cattle there and grew a few fields of hay and grain for feed as a part-time venture. He was employed full-time by an aerial photo mapping corporation with which, as it happened, I had done a considerable amount of business in the past. I was not acquainted with him, but I knew the company president quite well.

Fred called shortly after, and told me he'd just talked to the farm owner and that Frank, Judy, and I were welcome to join him for a hunt on his land at any time.

Fred and I then finalized our plans for the coming Saturday. Fred would come over at 6:00 AM. That would give us plenty of time for the thirty-five mile drive and to begin hunting at 7:00 A.M.

While we were having dinner, I informed Frank about our plan for the weekend. I told him that Fred had mentioned he'd bounced plenty of rabbits at that farm without a dog, and that the farm had probably not been hunted that fall. Frank said, "Well, if that's the case, Judy will have a ball." He was delighted that he'd not need to get up so early as when we drove to Pennsylvania.

When Saturday morning rolled around, I awakened at 4:30. No sooner did I turn on the kitchen light, when Judy began her Saturday morning serenade. Soon, Alice came to the kitchen and said, "You'd better go down there and get her before the neighbors start calling."

Soon after I brought her in, she went to Frank's room, jumped on his bed, and woke him with a few licks on his cheek. When he came to the kitchen he said, "She told me it's time to go hunting."

53

By the time we polished off our usual king-size breakfast and rounded up our gear, it was near 6:00 AM. Patsy, who'd been awakened by the commotion, held on to Judy while we stowed our gear in the car.

Fred had already come over and was waiting for us. The first thing he said was, "I could hear Judy howling more than an hour ago. No wonder the neighbors complain."

I laughed and said, "Well, she has a great voice, doesn't she? Just one of the benefits of living near a beagler."

On our drive, Fred told us a little about the terrain and other characteristics of the farm we planned to hunt. He said there were several pastures, and that the owner alternates his herd from one to the other. He went on to say that the owner would appreciate it if we would not go into the pasture where the cattle were feeding today.

I said, "We'll certainly comply with his wishes. Frank and I really appreciate his willingness to allow us to hunt."

With Fred's directions, in no time at all we pulled in at the farm. The sun was rising; a light frost which I knew would be gone in an hour or so, covered the ground.

Judy began to fuss impatiently. Frank put her on the leash lest she start out before we were ready.

As we loaded up I said, "Fred, you lead the way since you know the turf."

"Okay," he said. "Let's start right in on this pasture. There aren't any cattle here, it's pretty big, and there are lots of briar patches."

I immediately noticed that the close-cropped grasses contained a rich clover complement. There were indeed many small but very dense briar patches. This, I thought, was ideal. Rabbits certainly love clover, and they also love the security of dense briar patches. The spaces between them would offer clear shooting lanes.

Frank released Judy, and we started out through the pasture. I said to the guys, "There's plenty of open space here, so the chases will likely be long, wide circles."

We hadn't gone far, when Judy began to work at the edge of a small, thick briar patch. Presently, a rabbit scooted out on the opposite side. Judy heard him as he went out of the patch, then she looked up and saw him. She began to howl immediately as the rabbit ran down a slope toward an adjacent wooded area. She ran around the patch and pursued the rabbit by sight, steadily bawling all the way until they reached the woods. She then picked up the scent and continued her pursuit into heavy cover.

Fred had seen the whole exhibition. Amused, he said, "I thought for a moment she'd catch him."

I replied, "She really puts on a show when she sees one. Let's move ahead a little, spread out, and be ready when she brings him back."

From where I stood, I could clearly see down the slope to where the pasture abutted the woods. After what seemed a long wait, I saw the rabbit bust out of the cover thirty or more yards to the right of where it had gone in, and break into a fast run back up the slope. I said to the guys, "Be ready; he's coming back."

The rabbit ran about half-way from the woods to my position, then veered off to the right toward Frank. In a moment, I saw Frank throw down on him, follow through, and fire. Right away Frank yelled, "I got him, Dad!"

Judy, in the meantime, was close behind on the trail, continuing her steady bawl. Fred and I walked over to Frank's position where the three of us waited until she completed her chase, shook the rabbit a few times, laid it at Frank's feet, then sat and looked up as if to say, "It's time for my treat." Fred laughed as Frank rewarded her.

Fred remarked, "She hangs right in there and sticks to it, doesn't she? Never misses a beat."

We dressed and stowed the rabbit, and began to discuss the strategy for our next move.

"I think we should go back to where we started and hit some more of those briar clumps. There's bound to be another rabbit or two there," I said.

When the others agreed, we hastened back to where we'd begun and started once again to kick the patches. We moved off in a slightly different direction from the one we had pursued the first time.

By that time, all of the frost had lifted and the temperature had risen a few degrees. By observing Judy's behavior, I could see that she was picking up cold scent from the early morning hours in the close-cropped clover. I mentioned this to the others, and that the cold trails meant there were rabbits here somewhere.

It wasn't long before Judy began to yip at the edge of another of the many briar patches. She worked her way into the patch and began to bawl as she emerged from the other side. Back down the slope she went, toward the same wooded area as in the first chase.

"I didn't see that rabbit," Fred said.

"Nor did I," I replied. "Although, the area below the patch is fairly open. He must have sneaked out before we got this far. We'd better spread out again."

Fred moved over to my left, where a wagon road wound up the hill near the edge of the pasture. Frank moved to my right.

Not anxious to leave the protective cover, the rabbit bounced around in the patch for a good while. Judy continued her bawl without a pause. Realizing his futile

56

attempt to shake his pursuer, the rabbit finally broke into the open where he could run a good distance to the left of where he'd entered the thicket.

The rabbit continued to bear to the left in a wide semicircle. Then, by Judy's voice, I could tell that he'd started up the hill.

Presently, I saw Fred raise his hump-backed Browning semi-automatic in the direction of the wagon road and fire. When Fred yelled "I got him!", I motioned to Frank and we proceeded to Fred's position.

As we approached Fred, I saw his rabbit lying at the center of the wagon road. I said to Fred, "Go over now and stand a few feet from the rabbit until Judy comes up to him."

Soon after Fred stood by the rabbit, Judy completed the chase. To our astonishment, she looked up at Fred, then picked up the rabbit and ran back down the hill between the briar patches.

In a few minutes she trotted back, came to me, and looked up into my eyes.

"Judy," I said, "where's Fred's bunny?" She sat down, cocked her head a few times, and continued to look up. "Judy," I repeated, "where did you hide Fred's bunny?" Suddenly she rose to her feet, turned around, and began to walk back down the hill. I said to Fred, "Go back to where she picked up the rabbit and stand there."

"Frank," I said, "give Fred a couple of her treat biscuits." I then followed Judy down the hill. She looked back a few times to be sure I was following. When we'd walked thirty or forty yards, she stopped at the edge of a briar patch, put her nose down, and looked in.

I looked into the patch ahead of her, but saw nothing but the foot-high brown weeds, which did not appear disturbed, at the bottom of the briar stocks. Again I said,

"Judy, where did you hide Fred's bunny?" She looked up at me once more, then turned and took a step or two into the patch. She turned and looked up at me again, and then with her paw,she parted the grass, took a step backward, and looked up once again. There in the parted weeds ahead of her lay the lifeless rabbit. She backed away a few steps and looked up again.

"Bring him to me, Judy," I said. "Bring the bunny." She turned toward the rabbit, took a few steps forward, and picked it up. She turned again, brought the rabbit out, and laid it at my feet.

"Good girl," I said, while patting her on the head. As I picked up the rabbit I said, "Now let's go and give Fred his bunny." As I proceeded toward Fred, who'd remained in position, she proudly trotted along beside me.

Frank, who had followed us and observed what Judy had done, said, "Gosh, Dad, I can hardly believe it. Why do you suppose she did that?"

"Well, Buddy," I said, "let's hurry back to Fred and then I'll tell you what I think. But remember, it's only my theory. I could certainly be wrong."

When we came up to Fred, I laid the rabbit near his feet. "Judy," I said, "That's Fred's bunny. Give the bunny to Fred." Questioningly she looked up at me for a moment, then picked up the rabbit, took a few steps forward, and laid it at Fred's feet. Fred petted her and gave her the biscuits.

After we'd all had a good laugh and made quite a fuss over Judy, I attempted to rationalize what had happened. "Judy," I said, "has retrieved well since she was a puppy and this is only her second season. We've shot a good many rabbits in front of her and she's become accustomed to bringing them either to Frank or to me. I guess that's become second nature and she was just not about to bring the rabbit to anyone other than one of us."

"That may be so," Fred said, "but one thing's for sure. She's certainly a remarkable dog. The way she routs and weeds these rabbits out from dense cover is rare to say the least. And, the performance she just put on with this rabbit is something I've never heard of in all the years I've hunted."

"Neither have I," I said. "But then, nearly every time we hunt with her she seems to pull another trick from her sleeve. It keeps us wondering what's next."

While I helped Fred field dress his rabbit, Frank sat down in the grass with Judy and continued to praise and pet her.

After one more chase in the pasture, Frank shot his second rabbit for the day, noon was approaching, and the temperature had risen considerably. We took a lunch break, and gave Judy some water and a biscuit or two. We shed some clothes, and sat and talked for a while.

I asked Fred if he'd ever flushed a pheasant on this farm. "Not here," he said. "But, over the years I've seen a few on other farms nearby. Never had a decent shot at one, though."

As we made ready for the afternoon hunt, Fred suggested we hunt other parts of the farm. Frank and I agreed since we'd pretty well covered the pasture and adjacent areas.

It turned out to be quite a successful afternoon. By evening we'd each bagged a total of three rabbits for the day. The legal limit in Virginia was six per hunter, but I always liked to leave a few for seed, and I thought nine rabbits from that farm was enough for one day. I mentioned that to Fred, and he agreed that it was a good policy.

Judy had not hidden any more rabbits from Fred. At first, she hesitated for a moment in front of Fred with the bunny , but when she saw that I was watching, she laid them at his feet.

At one point at about mid-afternoon, Judy worked up a covey of quail in front of Fred. Fred shot a nice double, bringing down two birds. We'd have been hard pressed to find them in the tall weeds without Judy. One by one, she sniffed them out and brought them back to Fred.

On the short drive home, we relived each of the day's events as we customarily did. But, we knew that the incident of the hidden rabbit would be forever etched in our minds, and would be the subject of many stories in time to come.

In his younger days, Fred had been a volunteer fireman at the nearby community of McLean. He still stopped by the firehouse frequently to trade stories with old friends over a cup of coffee. During our conversation he said, "Wait 'till the boys at the firehouse hear this one. I can hardly wait to tell them."

"Unless some of them are beaglers," I said. "They may not believe it."

"They probably won't believe it whether they're beaglers or not," he replied. "If I hadn't seen it, I might not believe it either."

As we parted company on our arrival at home, Fred repeated what he'd told me several times that day. "That Judy's certainly one remarkable gun dog. Never before have I seen a dog perform like she did today. I hope you know how fortunate you are to have her. I'd give about anything to have one like her."

"They're hard to come by, Fred," I said proudly. "Awfully hard to come by."

CHAPTER VIII
THE NON-BELIEVER

A few years before Judy's time, on the commute to my office in Washington D.C., I met a former Pennsylvanian, Red Zaranski. Like myself, Red was a life long outdoorsman. He had grown-up in a rural setting in Western Pennsylvania, shooting rabbits over beagles as I had. When he came of age, he served our country, after which he came to Washington to pursue a career in engineering.

With all these things in common, Red and I became good friends. We swapped many stories on our daily hour long trips to and from the city.

On Monday mornings, Red listened with fascination while I re-lived our hunts of the previous weekends with particular emphasis on Judy's exemplary performance.

One Monday during the Pennsylvania small game season as I completed one of my tales, Red said, " I'd really like to see your dog run a rabbit. It's been a long time since I've hunted with a beagle."

He went on to say that some years earlier he'd come to know a farming family named Miller near Chambersburg, Pennsylvania, and had obtained permission to hunt with a companion or two on their property. He went there on a week-end once in a while he said, but since he had no dog, his hunts amounted to week-end hikes in the woods more than anything else.

Red had told me nostalgically of many boyhood hunts shared with relatives, friends, and their beagles. He'd often considered raising a beagle at his present home, but had not done so for fear that it's nocturnal howling might offend his neighbors.

I laughed and said "That's certainly a consideration all right." I told him that on numerous occasions I'd experienced that very problem.

"Anyway Red" I said, "Why don't you join Frank and me for a hunt next Saturday? We're always looking for new territory, so maybe we could give your friend's farm at Chambersburg a shot."

Red said "I'd really like that. Mr. Miller always complains about crop damage from large and small game, so I'm sure he'd be pleased to have their numbers reduced. I'll call and tell him we plan to be there early next Saturday morning."

"Fine," I said, "I'll look forward to it. We'll pick you up early on Saturday."

That evening during our dinner conversation, I mentioned to Frank my plan for us on the coming Saturday to hunt some new turf with my friend Red. Frank had met Red, liked him, and welcomed the idea of the new territory.

With amusement, I said to Frank "I wonder if Red shoots a rabbit, whether Judy will react in the same way as she did with our friend Fred Wenzel."

Frank laughed and said to his Mom and sister "You should have seen that. That was the funniest thing I ever saw. I told my friends about it, and some of them didn't even believe me."

Long before daylight on the following Saturday, Frank and I drove to Red's home, a distance of only a few miles. Red was ready and waiting. Frank and Judy got into the back seat, I helped Red stow his gear in the trunk, and we were off.

Judy was characteristically friendly with everyone. She jumped into the front seat and welcomed Red with a few licks until Frank called her to the back. She remained excited as she usually did for the entire trip.

Red said, "She certainly seems energetic and eager enough."

I replied, "She's always that way in the morning. As you'll see, in the evening after a hard day's hunt, she'll curl up the minute she's in the car and sleep until we get home."

By the time we reached our destination, daylight had broken. I was encouraged to see that the sky was overcast and the temperature was in the low 40's with minimum wind. The television weather forecast predicted light intermittent showers with no heavy precipitation.

Weather like that presents ideal small game hunting conditions. Scent holds well, and both hunter and dog are able to hunt aggressively without becoming either chilled or over heated. Sound carries well, enabling the hunter to track the chase at a long distance, and there is no glare from the sun, which has created difficulty for me on numerous occasions.

I scanned the surroundings as best I could. This farm of a few hundred acres appeared to be similar to the Morgan farm near Everett, but with more brushy areas not suitable for cultivation.

I said to Red "Now, you know the country here and Frank and I don't. So, you lead the way to the best game cover and we'll follow."

Red said "I'll try, but as I mentioned I've never hunted here with a dog, so there very well may be spots which harbor game that I've never been able to flush."

We started in at the border area with a thick stand of quaking aspen saplings and small briar patches interspersed.

We worked the cover very hard and after perhaps thirty minutes, while I was up to my neck in briars, I saw a rabbit scoot out ahead of me. I called Judy and put her on the trail. Then, I called to Frank and Red and advised them to get to the edge where they would have good shooting lanes.

Judy, by that time, had broken into a steady bawl as the rabbit ran far out ahead and broke into a wide arc to the left. Following Judy's sound, I could tell that the rabbit had turned abruptly to the left, and was heading back along the thicket edge where I hoped Frank and Red would be waiting. Presently, I heard the roar of Frank's 12 gauge. I waited for perhaps five minutes, when Judy's howling stopped. Then Frank called out "Dad I got him."

Happily, I made my way to Frank's position, arriving just as he stood his gun against a tree and prepared to dress the rabbit. I asked if he waited until Judy came up to the rabbit before he picked it up. "Yes," he said pointing to the briars. "The rabbit was in there, and she picked him up and brought him to me. I already gave her a treat."

"Excellent," I said as I held the rabbit up by it's hind legs. Frank unsheathed his buck knife and started the field dressing job, while Judy sat and waited patiently for her heart and liver reward.

Red soon found his way to our position. "Nice shot," he said to Frank. Then to me "That little dog certainly has a beautiful voice."

When the rabbit was tucked into Frank's game pocket, I said to Judy "Well let's go find another one."

She trotted off into the thicket, and we spread out and followed her.

We had two more chases that morning. Red missed a rabbit as it darted out ahead of him. Judy took up the chase immediately, but the rabbit soon holed up. After a while, Judy routed another, and brought him back around where I dumped him ten yards before he reached a hole.

I suggested to the others that we should take a break, and they agreed that we return to the car, have our lunch, and make ready for an afternoon hunt.

From his house, Mr. Miller had seen our car parked along the road. While we were finishing our lunch, he drove over on his tractor to swap a few tales.

Red promptly introduced him to Frank and me. He shook our hands with the impressive sincere grip of a man with a lifetime of honest hard work behind him. I immediately liked the elderly gentleman. He was jovial, outgoing, and hospitable. Although I'd never seen him before, by the time our lengthy conversation ended, I felt as though I'd known him for years.

Mr. Miller asked, "How'd you do this morning? I'm a little hard of hearing these days, but I thought I heard a few shots."

Frank promptly volunteered to tell him about the events of our morning hunt. He took it all in, and with a broad smile he turned to me and said, "That boy's quite the story teller. I'll bet he's a good shot too." I thanked him and confirmed that Frank was indeed a good shot.

Mr. Miller went on to say "I'm surprised you fella's didn't flush a few pheasants. I know they're here. I scared up a few while I was cutting corn. The rascals pull the stalks down and eat up bushels of it for me every year. The missus and I hear them crowing in the evening sometimes, and we see one once in a great while."

Soon Mr. Miller said "Well fellas I know you want to get back to your hunting and I've got to get back to my chores." We shook hands again, and thanked him for allowing us to hunt his property.

"Anytime," he said as he climbed up on his old John Deere. "Good luck this afternoon."

As Mr. Miller departed Frank, Red and I began our plan of attack for the afternoon hunt.

I told the others, "I'd really like to see if we could scare up a few pheasants this afternoon. I'd like for Red to see how Judy performs on a bird. Let's focus on the grain fields and adjacent areas. The game will likely move in to feed in the afternoon and evening."

When everyone agreed we loaded up, unleashed Judy, and began to move out. I said to Red, "Now you've hunted with beagles enough in the past that I assume you know what to do if she takes off on a bird."

"I've hunted rabbits with them many times," he replied, "but not pheasants."

I had already explained the procedure to him, but I went over it again. "Try to keep up with her as best you can," I said.

I had parked at the edge of a field which appeared to have been a pasture, but where there were no cattle on that day. The field was probably one hundred fifty yards long, half that wide, and consisted of closely cropped grass with many high weed clumps and a loose briar patch here and there. The far end of the field abutted a large cut corn field where only the stubble and a few fallen stalks remained.

"Let's work our way across this pasture toward the corn field," I said. With the three of us abreast, Frank in the center, Red on the left and I on the right, and Judy five to ten yards ahead, we moved out.

We had progressed about one half the length of the field when I noticed Judy had slowed down, and from the movement of her tail I knew she was picking up scent. I raised my hand and to my companions and said "She's on to something. Let's give her a chance to work it out."

Soon, Judy began to yip as she moved forward in a straight line. As her speed increased, her voice changed from the yip to her familiar bawl. I said "She's on a bird now. Try to keep up with her. Frank, come this way a bit so you and Red are equally spaced behind her. I'll keep over to the right so as not to interfere with your shot or Red's."

When Judy had progressed to within twenty-five yards of the end of the field, she reduced her speed, but continued to move ahead very stealthily. Soon, she stopped and crouched at the edge of a thick clump of grass four or five feet wide. As it happened, Red had stopped running and was standing at the opposite side of the same clump, a bit winded from his run.

I said "Watch it now Red. There's a bird there in front of you."

"What?" he said, "There's no bird there. If there was, I could see it."

I said, "There's a bird there all right. You'd better be ready."

Suddenly, Judy pounced and an angry cock bird ascended toward the cloudy sky, so close to Red that I thought for a moment it would strike him in the face.

Red, in his astonishment, nearly lost his balance and fell over backward. As the bird leveled off and went into a straight forward flight, Red regained his bearing and emptied his 12 bore pump gun. But by that time, the bird was pretty far out and Red's shots fell short. Frank also managed to crank off a shot which only caused the bird to shift into a higher gear. Since I considered that a shot from my position would be unsafe, I did not fire.

Red was completely taken aback by what had happened. As I began to laugh, he said "Boy, I've never seen anything like that in my life. If I hadn't seen it happen I wouldn't believe it. That bird sat right there just a few feet from me and I never saw it. Why couldn't I see it? And why didn't it fly or run before I got that close?"

Frank said "Yeah Dad, I never saw one sit that tight before."

"Guys," I said "they just seem to have an uncanny way of concealing themselves. Although they rarely sit that tight, they occasionally do. You just never know when. They're full of surprises. Red, just think of how many you've probably walked by without a hint of their presence while tramping around up here without a dog."

"Probably a good many," he replied, "but I'll tell you one thing. I won't doubt that dog of yours again. She certainly knows what she's doing."

"She sure does," Frank said as he patted Judy affectionately.

After a good laugh, and plenty of praise toward Judy, we resumed our afternoon hunt, moving on into the corn field.

We ran after and flushed two more pheasants in that big field. One was a hen, and the other was a nice rooster which I brought down after Red missed.

"I must not be giving those birds enough lead," Red said. "I could swear my aim was just ahead of that one."

"They fly faster than you might think," I said. "Your lead, of course, has to vary with the direction of the flight." I mentioned what I'd told Frank long ago. "Remember to swing through and shoot where you think he's going to be when the shot gets there, and not where he is now."

Judy routed three more rabbits that afternoon. I was pleased to see that Red shot well and scored on two of them, and Frank bagged the third.

With all the excitement, I hadn't realized it was getting late. When I looked at my watch I said "Well guys, we'd better pack it in for today. By the time we make our way to the car it will be almost dark."

"Frank," I said, "We'd better put Judy on the leash. If we don't, she's liable to find another scent, and it's too late for a chase."

After stowing our gear in the car, I drove over to Mr. Miller's house. Each of us thanked him for a great hunt on his farm that day. We offered him a couple of our rabbits, but he declined the offer saying "The missus doesn't like to cook them anymore. She says they're always full of BBs. I used to hunt them, but I haven't brought one in for years."

Mrs. Miller invited us in for coffee and a piece of the pie she'd just lifted from the oven. It was tempting, but we graciously declined. The hour was late, we had a long drive ahead, and our families would be concerned.

When we parted company, Mr. Miller said in his sincere country voice, "You fellas come back anytime." We thanked him again and said we sincerely hoped we would.

On our journey home as Frank and Judy slept soundly in the back seat, Red and I talked over the day's hunt. Red told me repeatedly how appreciative he was that we'd taken him along. He couldn't get over how well Judy had performed.

On Monday mornings as we rode the bus to our offices, Red and I usually fell into conversation with a group of friends. Each of us told the story of our weekend adventures. Some of the guys were golfers, some were baseball or football enthusiasts, and so on.

On that Monday following our hunt at Mr. Miller's farm, Red was at the center of the stage. His audience listened attentively as he recalled each detail of last Saturday's hunt. They were most impressed and fascinated, and glanced at each other in wonder as he recounted the outstanding performance of our great gun dog "Judy."

Frank III, and Judy -- The Training Ground -- McLean, Virginia

Frank III and his second pheasant -- The Old Home Place --

Patsy, Judy and friends -- The Old Home Place -- Reynoldsville, Pennsylvania

Frank III and Judy -- Our Pennsylvania daily limit -- The McNabb Farm -- Gettysburg, Pennsylvania

Judy and a briar patch rabbit -- The Miller Farm -- Chambersburg, Pennsylvania

Judy in pursuit -- The Honeysuckle Patch -- Loudoun County, Virginia

Judy -- A short break after a long chase -- Loudoun County, Virginia

Judy and the stone fence pheasant – The Morgan Farm -- Everett, Pennsylvania

75

CHAPTER IX
JUDY'S PUPPIES

When Judy became four years old and in the prime of her life, she had proven her mettle under every condition imaginable. She had hunted well in very dry weather, in rain, and in snow. Many scores of rabbits, many pheasants, a few quail, and even a few ruffed-grouse had been brought down in front of her.

She had gained a distinctive reputation by that time, largely because Frank and I had taken many friends with us on our weekend hunts. Being impressed with her hunting skills, the friends of course, told others, and soon the stories became widespread among local hunters.

Around that time, I began to consider having Judy bred. Several friends expressed interest in buying puppies, and of course, I'd planned to keep at least one, or perhaps a pair.

Judy, as I pointed out in an earlier chapter, was a thoroughbred. To this day her five-generation pedigree hangs on the wall of my library. As I mentioned earlier, she had descended from the highly-renowned and much sought-after Pearson Creek bloodline. Therefore, my plan was to locate a distinguished Pearson Creek male for the breeding.

During recent conversations with my old friends, Mike Campana and Ralph McGuire, I learned that all of Judy's siblings had become field trial champions. Mike and Ralph urged me to start running her in field trials. "If we lived near a club where the trials were held," I told them, "I may have considered that. But with my situation, I prefer to spend my limited free time hunting with Judy and my son."

In my old hometown in Pennsylvania, there lived an elderly gentleman named Calvin Becker, who was well known in beagler circles. Calvin reportedly owned a pure-bred Pearson Creek male named Jack, who had gained quite a reputation as a field trial champion, as a gun dog, and as a stud dog.

Calvin, I knew, was a close friend of my old buddy, Friz Harmon. I called Friz and asked if he could arrange a breeding between Judy and Jack.

A few days later Friz returned my call. He told me he'd talked with Calvin, and that he was agreeable. Calvin happened to be familiar with both Judy's dam (mother), her sire (father), and with her field champion siblings. Friz went on to say that Calvin had known my family well and remembered me when I was a boy. Customarily, there is a substantial breeding fee associated with these thoroughbred dogs. But, Calvin asked only that he should keep one of the puppies in payment.

I told Friz that I agreed to that arrangement, and when the proper time came I would bring Judy to Reynoldsville.

It was during winter when that arrangement was made. Judy, I had noticed, was in estrus in winter and again in the spring. My family and I then planned for a trip to Reynoldsville when the time was right.

On our trips to our old home territory, we nearly always took Judy with us. At the halfway point of the six hour drive, we usually stopped for dinner at a restaurant called the Gateway in Breezewood, Pennsylvania. After dinner, we always bought a hamburger for Judy, and after a few trips she came to expect it.

Beagles, more than many breeds, are overly attracted to food, mainly because of their intense sense of smell. After dinner when we approached our car where Judy waited, she immediately began to jump from one seat to the other in anticipation of her treat.

Knowing how excitedly Judy wolfed her food down, Frank and Patsy never could be talked into feeding her from their hands, fearing that their fingers might get nipped. They watched in amusement as Alice bravely volunteered, expecting her to be bitten at any moment. Amazing as it was, in all the trips we made during Judy's lifetime, not once was Alice ever bitten. As the old adage goes, Judy "never bit the hand that fed her."

On the morning following our arrival in Reynoldsville; Frank, Friz, Judy, and I proceeded to Calvin's home. On our arrival, we immediately heard the howling of beagles from the back of the house as Calvin's three dogs--Jack, and a pair of females--winded Judy. Frank leashed Judy, and he and I walked to the backyard as Friz went to rouse

Calvin. As we approached the kennels, looking at Jack, I said, "Wow, Frank, what a handsome dog."

"He really is," Frank said. "Will he be the father of our puppies?"

"That's what we're hoping for," I said, as Calvin and Friz appeared.

After a warm handshake and a few brief stories about my grandfather, who'd been a friend of Calvin's, we began to discuss the plan of action.

Calvin had an old, single stall garage where he kept bales of straw for the dog kennels, garden tools, etc. His plan was to lock Jack and Judy in the garage for a while, to allow them to go about their romance and mating game without distraction. He had spread a thick layer of straw on the dirt floor so that the dogs could lie down comfortably if they so desired.

First, we put Judy in the garage. Then, we cracked the door open enough for Jack to squeeze in. With a whiff of Judy's scent, Jack hurried in without persuasion. Calvin had removed a high window in the side of the garage so that he could look in and determine whether or not everything was going well.

Soon, we heard a terrific commotion from inside the garage, and a cloud of dust began to pour out of the vacant window space. Calvin and I peered through the dust to behold Judy angrily chasing Jack in circles on the floor of the garage, bawling all the while, and creating more dust as the chase continued. At one point, she caught up with him, and bit him on the backside, causing him to emit a cry of pain.

With a worried look, Frank asked, "Dad, is Judy all right?"

I laughed and said, "Sure, she's okay Buddy, but I'm not so sure about Jack."

Calvin said, "I've had similar situations before, but I don't think I ever saw a female quite that feisty. One of us may have to go in and get them settled down."

Friz was quick to volunteer. He said, "I'm an old hand at this. I've experienced it many times and I know just what to do. The problem is, Jack is strange to Judy. I'll go in there and get them settled and acquainted. Then, I'll get down on the floor and draw them together slowly. Soon they'll be licking each other on the face, and the first thing you know, they'll mate."

"Go to it," I said. "But be careful when you go in that the dogs don't get out."

Friz cracked the door open enough to slip inside. By this time, Judy had backed Jack into a corner. She stood a few feet away, sounding off in a scolding voice. Friz took hold of both dogs by their collars, got down on his knees, and attempted to bring them together and under control.

Suddenly, a loud ruckus began again and another cloud of dust shot out of the window hole. We looked in on a sight to behold. Friz and the two dogs were rolling around, under and on top of one another, with Friz trying desperately to keep hold of their collars. Friz had come down with a severe attack of hay fever from the straw dust, and was sneezing and coughing incessantly.

Finally, Friz let go of the collars and managed to get on his feet. He hastened to the door, and when he opened it, Jack ran out with Judy in close pursuit.

Across the yard they went, and into a neighbor's garden. Frank, Calvin, and I immediately took up the chase, calling to the dogs as we ran. Friz was incapacitated by his hay fever attack and unable to follow. Finally, we caught up with them when Jack took refuge under a neighbor's back porch, with Judy there baying like a coon dog which had just treed a ringtail.

During the chase, we traversed four or five backyards and gardens. Luckily, Calvin's neighbors were good-natured, rural, Pennsylvania folks, and were accustomed to the antics of beagles.

Frank leashed Judy while I crawled under the porch, brought Jack out, and leashed him for Calvin. "I've seen all kinds of things in my time," said Calvin as he struggled to regain his breath. "But I've never seen a little female act like that before."

We returned to Calvin's yard to find Friz sitting in a lawn chair, gasping and trying, in vain, to stop sneezing. Mrs. Becker had come out to investigate the commotion and had brought Friz a glass of water and a dampened towel to wipe his face.

Both Calvin and Friz were of an advanced age, and had owned beagles nearly all of their lives. They agreed that in rare cases there are females which simply refuse to breed. They had both seen it happen in the past they said, and perhaps, they thought Judy was unfortunately one of those. They agreed, however, that they'd never before seen a female that adamant about it. Frank, who was taking all of this in, spoke up and said, "Judy seems to be pretty determined about everything."

That being said, we all had a good laugh, even though we were somewhat disappointed with the outcome of the day's events. We shook hands with Calvin, thanked him for his efforts, and departed. By that time Friz had substantially recovered from his debilitating hay fever attack.

In a few days, we returned to our home in Virginia and resumed our normal routine. Friends and acquaintances, who had expressed interest in Judy's puppies, were disappointed, but quite amused to hear my story of the breeding attempt.

We continued to run Judy at our training ground, and spent time at the trap range, in preparation for the approaching fall hunting seasons. By this time, Frank had become an excellent shot at the range, breaking many birds without a miss, and winning more praise from my old friend Phil Godfrey.

In Judy's time, the small game hunting season in Virginia began in mid-October and continued through the holidays and into the New Year. Pennsylvania had two seasons. The early season spanned the month of November. The late season came in soon after Christmas and lasted several weeks. Hunters were therefore given plenty of time to hunt in diverse weather conditions.

Until the year we attempted to have Judy bred, we never took her to the woods during the late Pennsylvania season because she was in estrus at that time. However, since our effort to have her bred had been disastrous, and the beagle authorities whom I relied upon had advised me that she probably wouldn't breed, Frank and I decided to extend our time afield into the late Pennsylvania season.

Soon after the late season began, we drove to our favorite grounds, the McNabb farm, for a day's hunt. When we arrived, the ground was covered with a light coat of snow, which began to disappear with the rising temperature later in the morning.

We had two chases fairly early. Frank shot one rabbit, and the other holed up. At about mid-morning, Judy routed another rabbit and commenced her third chase of the day. After perhaps fifteen minutes had passed, her howling abruptly ceased. I said to Frank, "He probably holed. Let's just wait here until she comes back."

After an unusually long wait, I said, "That's odd. She should be back by now." I waited a few more minutes and then began to call her. Having called numerous times to no avail, we became concerned.

Finally I said, "I guess we'd better go look for her."

When we last heard her, she was about a one hundred yards ahead and beginning to bear left in some heavy cover. Not far on the opposite side of the cover, was the McNabb property line. Close beyond the line were several houses, and I could hear the barking of other dogs in that vicinity.

"Frank," I said, "Let's spread out to about twenty yards between us and move rather quickly toward where we last heard her. Try to keep in sight of me as we move."

Just as we began to move out, Frank yelled excitedly, "Dad, here she comes!" I quickly looked to the right, and lo and behold, there came Judy, proudly trotting along toward Frank, accompanied by a cute, little black-and-white male mixed breed.

"Oh, boy," I said. "I think we might have a problem. Put her on the leash as quickly as you can." Frank called her, and she started toward him. Apparently frightened, the little male turned and began to run away. Judy turned to follow him, but Frank managed to catch her and put her on the leash.

"What do you suppose happened, Dad?" Frank asked. "You don't think she mated with that dog, do you? After what she did up in Reynoldsville, and after what Calvin and Friz told us, I thought she wouldn't mate."

With a laugh, I said, "Well, Buddy, it sort of looks like the authorities might have been mistaken this time. I hope not, but we'll know before long. Let's keep her on the leash until after lunch. Then, we'll hunt a few more hours on another part of the farm."

Our lunch conversation that day consisted mostly of our story about trying to have Judy bred, and about her love affair with the little black-and-white pooch that morning. Jean and Sam were quite amused, and we all had a good laugh.

Soon I said to Frank, "Well, we'd better get out there and hunt for a while. We may be forced to quit early. That sky looks ominous and the wind is picking up. It looks like there's a storm brewing."

By mid-afternoon, the temperature had dropped considerably. A hard snow squall had come up and the wind velocity had increased. By that time, Judy had routed two rabbits, one of which I shot. The second one holed up soon after the chase began.

I said, "I don't think the rabbits will run in this storm. The ones which aren't already holed up will likely be anxious to do so soon after they're routed. Are you ready to pack it in?"

Frank confirmed that he was ready. He leashed Judy, and we headed for the car.

By the time we got there, the storm had escalated to a full-scale blizzard. We hurriedly stowed our gear, said a brief good-bye to Jean and Sam, and were on our way toward home.

Alice and Patsy were greatly amused with the story of Judy's romance with the little black-and-white male. "It seems," I said, "that our thoroughbred Judy, of acclaimed lineage, has spurned the courtship of noble blue-blood Jack to favor the affections of a riff-raff mutt."

With obvious hopefulness Patsy asked, "Do you think she'll have puppies? When will they be born? And what will we do with them?"

I said, "We probably won't know for a few weeks, If she has puppies, they'll arrive in a few months. Since they won't be thoroughbreds, we'll have to find good homes for them and give them away."

I was pleased that neither Frank nor Patsy expressed interest in keeping any. That being the case, I'd be spared the task of trying to talk them out of it, or so I thought.

As the weeks went by it became obvious by Judy's appearance that she would, in fact, be giving birth to a litter of puppies. So, we began to make preparations for the new arrivals. Alice arranged a comfortable place in the basement where they'd be born, and Judy would nurse them.

Don Tarchak, a friend in Pennsylvania who was a rabbit hunter, and had seen Judy run rabbits on one occasion, had expressed interest in a female puppy if I should have Judy bred. He had never owned a thoroughbred, but he and his father had always hunted with mixed breeds which were part beagle. Some of them, he said, had turned out to be pretty decent gun dogs. So, when it was confirmed that we'd have a litter, I called Don and promised one to him.

In the meantime, Frank and Patsy had talked to friends who'd like to have puppies, and had gotten permission from their parents. Thus, the puppies were spoken for long before they were born.

One Saturday morning, during the final days of the gestation period, Frank and Patsy were visiting friends, and I had range officer duty at our sportsman's club. Prior to leaving home, I mentioned to Alice that I expected the puppies to born any day now. She said she would look in on Judy periodically while I was gone.

Near noon that day I returned home. As I turned into the driveway Alice ran out to meet me. "Hurry," she said. "The puppies are here." We hastened to the basement where Judy laid on her blanket, contentedly nursing four delightful little puppies. She had given birth to seven, but unfortunately, three were still-born. Two of the puppies had pronounced beagle markings. One was nearly solid black and the other nearly all white.

Judy was adamantly protective of her puppies. More than a week would pass before she would allow any of us to touch them. But in good time, Frank, Patsy, and their friends began to spend many hours playing with them, and they soon became accustomed to people.

As I anticipated, when the time came that the puppies were weaned and ready for adoption, both of the kids had become attached to them and asked if they might keep just one. I reminded them that we had already promised the puppies to our friends and we could not break our promises.

The kids' friends, who had anxiously awaited the moment, came for their puppies. My family and I met Don and his family half-way between our homes where we presented their puppy to them. We were satisfied then that they all had good homes.

In time to come, Don would tell me that his puppy had turned out to be a reasonably good hunter. To at least some extent, she had inherited Judy's genes.

We were greatly disappointed that because of Judy's romantic inclinations, we were denied thoroughbred puppies. Frank and I discussed this at great length. Finally, our disappointment was overshadowed by the realization that Judy was now in her prime, and to our good fortune, we'd probably hunt with her for another six or seven years. By that time Frank would be a grown man, pursuing a life and career of his own. We'd wait and see what our circumstances would be at that time.

We talked of the countless experiences afield that we'd shared during the past few years. With amusement, we chalked up the breeding experience as one more adventure. We looked forward to many more great adventures in the company of our super gun dog, Judy.

CHAPTER X
THE FLAT ROCK RABBIT

When circumstances permitted, my family and I drove to western Pennsylvania each fall to spend much of the Thanksgiving week with relatives. We took Judy with us, of course, and Frank and I had the opportunity to hunt with some of my old friends and relatives.

In Judy's fifth year, while planning our Thanksgiving trip, I decided to call my great friend and life-long mentor, Guido Malacarne, whom I've always referred to as "Mal," and arrange for us to get together for a hunt one day during that week. Mal had hunted with us on an occasion when Judy was younger and was impressed with her skills.

Mal is a very accomplished man. He's a combat veteran of World War II, a former educator, a hall of fame athlete, retired Chief Executive Officer of a major corporation, a world-class big game hunter, and a truly inspirational man. In all the years I've hunted, I can truthfully say Mal is the most intense hunter I've ever known. While I was a high school student, he was my guidance counselor and geography teacher. He's always said that when I came along he decided there were better ways to make a living, and he resigned from teaching. He and his lovely wife, Janice, reside to this day near my family home in Pennsylvania.

Over the years, Mal had owned thoroughbred beagles, and I was privileged to have hunted with some of them. The most memorable one was a male named Bob. Old Bob, as I remember, could find a rabbit where one would swear there weren't any.

When I talked with Mal and we arranged for a day's hunt, he told me he knew an area not far from his home which had always yielded rabbits in previous years, but he had not yet hunted it during that particular year. He went on to say that the land was posted, but he knew the owner quite well and he'd obtained permission to hunt there some years earlier. Probably, he added, that since it was posted, no one else had hunted it in recent years either.

"Sounds like the place to go," I said.

We planned to meet very early on the designated day. Mal thought it would take an entire morning to thoroughly hunt that area, and he knew some other good patches that we might try in the afternoon.

When I relayed the plan to Frank, he was quite enthused. He had enjoyed hunting with Mal on numerous occasions, both for small game and for deer. Frank had decided he'd like to try hunting with a pump action gun that season. The pump action worked much differently than the breach loaders he was accustomed to. It took some familiarization, but he soon got the hang of it, and became a reasonably good shot.

On the day of our hunt, we polished off a hardy breakfast prepared by my Aunt Lois, whom our kids referred to as "Gram." We had boarded Judy in a vacant kennel owned by Gram's neighbor and friend, and at daybreak, Frank went after her and brought her on the leash.

By that time, Mal had arrived and had come in for a cup of coffee. After a story or two, we began to stow our gear. A light rain began to fall and Gram said, "It must be lots of fun is all I can say, to go out and tramp around in the rain all day."

In the meantime, Judy had begun her hunting morning serenade, and Frank expressed concern that she'd waken Gram's neighbors. I said, "It's okay, Buddy. It's different here from where we live. These folks are well-accustomed to beagles."

Soon we drove off to the hunting ground which was only a few miles away. The rain proved intermittent and had ceased by the time we arrived. The temperature was just a few degrees above freezing.

The grounds we were about to hunt had been farmland thirty or more years earlier. The present owner had operated an open pit (strip) mine there during the World War II period and for a few years thereafter. At that time, coal was needed urgently to fuel the production of our war machinery. Strip mining, to a great extent, replaced deep mining since coal could be extracted more rapidly with a fraction of the manpower.

The mine operators of that period weren't required to post bond as a guarantee that the "cuts" would be backfilled and reforested. They were, however, required to pay a penalty for failing to carry out the land reclamation process. In most cases, it was less expensive to pay the fine and move on than to reclaim the land. Consequently, to this day, much of the land in western Pennsylvania bears scars from the strip mining of that period.

On the positive side, the soil in the open cuts is apparently conducive to the growth of dense briars and wild grapevine thickets. To the good fortune of the hunter, that kind of vegetation produces excellent rabbit and other game habitat and feed.

As we started in at the entrance to one of the longer cuts, I said, "We're going to have to rely heavily on Judy. The briars and vines are nearly impenetrable here. But, if there are rabbits anywhere they're bound to be here."

As Judy eagerly waded into the cover, the three of us spread out across the cut. I took the center position, with Mal on my right near the high wall, and Frank on my left at the edge of the cut.

Judy was a few yards directly ahead of me. She immediately began to sniff the ground while she worked hard to penetrate the cover. I could tell she was picking up old scent, and I called to Mal, "There are rabbits here all right. She's cold trailing already."

Within a few minutes, I caught a glimpse of a rabbit scooting out five yards ahead of Judy. She saw the rabbit and immediately started to bawl as the chase began. I called to Frank and reminded him that in this kind of cover the rabbit normally runs short circles, and is not far ahead of the dog.

The rabbit ran a complete short circle within the cover. On the second time around as it swung right toward the high wall, I heard the report of Mal's semi-automatic 12 gauge. A few minutes later Mal shouted, "I got him."

I made my way through the cover to Mal's position and held the rabbit while he field dressed it. We agreed to continue to advance in our original positions clear to the end of the cut, since there was plenty of rabbit sign and the cover was promising.

I returned to my position, and we began to move forward again. Judy began again to work her way through the cover a few yards directly ahead of me.

We hadn't gone far until we were confronted with a thick tangle of grape vines. Soon after she entered the vines, Judy began to work back and forth rapidly. From her familiar short yips, I surmised that a bird was about to be flushed. I alerted Frank and Mal, then attempted to follow Judy into the entanglement. In only a moment, a pair of ruffed-grouse noisily took to the air and leveled off in their characteristic, erratic flight. I managed to discharge both barrels, but did not touch a feather. Mal had caught sight of the birds in flight, but by that time they were out of shotgun range.

The ruffed-grouse, the Pennsylvania state bird, is one of the most difficult targets for two reasons. Firstly, they are normally found only in very dense cover, such as grapevine or thorn apple thickets. Secondly , their flight is usually very erratic, presenting a difficult follow-through and lead for the shot-gunner. Among Pennsylvania hunters there's an old saying:"If you bring down two birds with a box of ammunition (twenty five shots), you've had a successful day's hunt." The ruffed-grouse is often referred to by the nickname "thunderbird," because they create a thunderous noise by the flapping of their wings in flight.

As we moved on through the cover, it was evident that there was an abundance of game thereabout. There was plenty of sign to be seen, and Judy worked continuously.

Soon, as she began to bawl up ahead, we knew that another rabbit had been routed. After hopping back and forth in the nearly impenetrable cover, the rabbit broke out to the left in Frank's direction. In a few moments, he cranked off two shots with his pump gun. Right away he called out, "Dad, I missed him. He's still running."

When in a few more moments Judy stopped howling, I assumed that the rabbit had holed. I called to Frank, "Can you see Judy?"

He replied, "No, she's too far up ahead." Since Judy had not come back to me, I walked over to Frank and asked him to show me where he'd last seen her.

Frank and I started to walk in the direction Judy had gone, and soon I could see her up ahead, digging and scratching at a rock right at the edge of the cut.

"There she is," I said. "Looks like you winged that rabbit and he crawled under a rock." As we continued toward Judy, I yelled to Mal, "We have a rabbit under a rock over here."

Mal arrived at the rock soon after Frank and I did. We decided that Frank would hold Judy back, and Mal and I would try to lift the rock away. The rock was large, flat, and very heavy. So, we all laid our guns down, and Frank pulled Judy back and held her by the collar while Mal and I moved the rock.

To our dismay, there was no rabbit to be seen. Judy, in the meantime, was squealing and straining to get back to where the rock had been. "I don't understand that," I said. "She's never been wrong before."

"She's not wrong this time, either," Mal said. "You can bet there's a rabbit there somewhere."

Suddenly, Judy turned to the left and began to bawl furiously. As Mal turned he yelled, "Hey, there goes the rabbit."

Out of nowhere it seemed, a rabbit had appeared and began to run like greased lightening along the edge of the cut. Frank let go of Judy's collar, and the chase was on. We all stood gaping with our guns lying on the ground.

"We'd better hurry and get spread out," Mal said. "My guess is that rabbit will soon try to get back to the thick cover." He then hastened to his position near the high wall. Frank and I each found spots where we could see reasonably well.

In ten or fifteen minutes, we knew from the sounds of Judy that the rabbit was heading back. It seemed to be heading in Mal's direction, and sure enough we soon heard his shot ring out, followed by, "I got him."

Frank and I arrived at Mal's position at about the same time as Judy did. She went about her ritual, picking up the rabbit and shaking it a few times before laying it at Mal's feet. Then, she turned and began to run back toward the rock we had moved without waiting for her treat.

"Judy," I called, "come back here. We got the bunny. Come on back and get your treat."

When she paid no attention, I began to go after her. Mal said, "Wait a minute. I know where she's headed. Let's follow her."

Judy led us right back to the flat rock where she began to scratch and whine again. "Judy," I said, "we shot the bunny. There's no bunny there." I attempted to pull her away, but she went right back.

"There's a rabbit there somewhere," Mal said.

I said, "There can't be. I could see it if there was."

"Now, I taught you better than that," he said. "She wouldn't be there scratching at that rock if there wasn't one there. Take a good look where that rock was."

With a closer examination I found that there was another flat rock underneath where the big one had been, partly covered with dirt. Mal looked down and said, "Look, there's a small hole at the far edge. See if you can up-end that rock."

As I attempted to scrape away the dirt that held the rock in place, I said, "Are you kidding? That hole isn't big enough for a chipmunk."

But when I managed to lift the rock away, there, before our eyes, lay a lifeless rabbit. Judy at once picked it up, shook it a few times, and laid it at our feet. She proudly looked up at me.

"I should have known better than to doubt her after some of the things we've seen her do," I said. "But I still don't see how that rabbit got through a hole that small."

"Frank," I said, "just as we thought, you winged that rabbit and he took refuge under the rock." As I turned to Mal I asked, "But where do you suppose the rabbit you shot came from?"

"I've no idea," he said. "He must have been nesting right behind us. In this kind of weather, they'll often sit tight like that. But when Judy started to run back toward that rock, even though it was a good distance away, I knew right then there were two different rabbits. She's an exceptional hunter. My advice is don't ever doubt her again."

We continued to push through the long cut that morning. Judy bounced two more rabbits. I shot one and the other holed. Judy worked a grouse up in front of Frank, and he brought it down with the first shot. We were all excited about that, and Mal and I shook his hand and congratulated him on his first grouse.

By noon, the temperature had dropped a few degrees and the light showers had turned to snow flurries. We all agreed it was time for a lunch break.

While we were having lunch in the car, Mal said, "We've pretty well covered this patch, but I know a few other ones that should be productive. One of them is not far from here."

From the backseat, where he was sharing a sandwich with Judy, Frank asked, "Can we go to another old strip mine?"

With a chuckle Mal said, "You like those old strip mines, do you?"

"Yes," Frank said. "They're full of game."

"Well," said Mal, "I think we can find another one nearby."

After a short drive following Mal's instructions, I proceeded up a dirt road for roughly a mile. I could see several old strip mine cuts on the hillside to our right.

Pointing to an old access road to one of the cuts, Mal said, "Pull in right there. There are three or four overgrown cuts here. They're not as long as the one we hunted this morning, but I doubt that we can cover all of them in one afternoon."

Our afternoon hunt was quite successful. The old mine cuts were thickly overgrown and yielded a fair amount of game, just as the one we'd hunted in the morning. Judy bounced three rabbits, and each of us bagged one. To my pleasant surprise, she had no hole-ups.

Judy flushed three single grouse that afternoon. I pulled off a lucky shot and brought down the first one. I missed the second, and Frank missed the third. As darkness began to creep in, we agreed to call it a day and head for home.

When we pulled in at the old homestead, Frank immediately went about feeding Judy and getting her secured for the night.

Mal and I went in for a hot cup of coffee, and Frank joined us as soon as he'd taken care of Judy. As we each savored a piece of warm pie which Gram had just lifted from the oven, we relived the events of the thoroughly enjoyable and rewarding hunt of that day. The highlights, of course, were Frank's first grouse and the rabbit under the rock. He proudly showed his grouse to Gram, and we all congratulated him again.

As he made ready to depart, Mal said, "That's an exceptional little dog you have. Best I've hunted with since old Bob. Have you ever considered having her bred?"

He laughed heartily when, in summary, we recounted the breeding effort we'd experienced. The fact that he was well-acquainted with our beagle authorities, Friz and Calvin, made the story all the more amusing.

As Frank and I shook hands with my old friend and he departed, I said, "It certainly was a great day. I'm glad we could get together. Let's do it again soon."

"Call me when you're ready," Mal said. "And take good care of Judy. You'll be hard-pressed to find another one like her."

CHAPTER XI
THE GENERAL'S POINTERS

The abundance of small game varies from season to season as a result of many factors. If the previous winter had been mild, the survival rate of rabbits and birds would have been greater of course, than in the aftermath of a severe winter. If the rate of rainfall in the early spring is abnormally high, many young rabbits and game birds drown in their nests. In an exceptionally dry year, feed and cover so essential to wildlife populations lack in abundance.

Other factors such as uncontrolled predation, loss of habitat, and disease also contribute to a scarcity of game. A certain amount of predation is essential however because in a situation where game is over-populated, the animals are more susceptible to contagious disease.

98

The variation in game abundance is, of course, very noticeable to the small game hunter. Areas with a high game yield one year may not be productive at all in the next. In summary, a perfect balance of nature from year to year is rare.

One of the years during which Frank, Judy and I hunted extensively in Southern Pennsylvania comes to mind. The conditions that year all seemed conducive to plentiful game. We hunted mainly on three different farms and enjoyed great success on each hunt. We filled our freezer with rabbits and birds, and gave many of both to neighbors and friends.

Judy was overworked that year. From the time we arrived at the hunting grounds until quitting time, she was running a rabbit or working up a bird almost continuously. It was one of the most fruitful years in all of my small game hunting experience.

To our delight, the pheasant population seemed to be at an all-time high. Frank and I literally ran our legs off following Judy's pursuit of the wily birds, and between hunts we made many trips to the local sporting goods store to replenish our ammunition.

Prior to the beginning of the season, Frank had decided that he'd like to try the double barrel that year. So, he hunted with my old trusty 12 gauge side by side, while I carried a superposed double barrel. As the season progressed, he became more adept with the double barrel and declared it was his favorite. He liked the idea of the full and modified choke combination as well as the sight rib.

One perfectly gorgeous November day that year, after a successful morning hunt on the north section of the McNabb farm, Frank and I were headed back to the farmhouse as the noon hour approached. Our game pockets were heavily laden, mostly with rabbits, but we had each bagged a pheasant as well.

As we walked across an ankle high hayfield on high ground, I looked off to our half right and saw a hunter with two large dogs approaching us at a distance of roughly seventy-five yards. When the hunter waved, we stopped. I returned the wave, then leashed Judy.

Immediately, I identified the hunter as one Thomas O'Brian, an elderly, retired Air Force General whom I'd met a few years earlier at the McNabb farmhouse. As in our case, the general was one of the few who were privileged to hunt the McNabb farm. He was accompanied that morning by a pair of tall, elegant looking, German short haired pointers.

"Morning General," I said as he and his dogs drew near. "Good to see you out this beautiful day. How was your morning hunt?"

"Well," he said, "The dogs worked up a couple of birds for me. I got a shot off at one of them, but I guess I was stretching the gun barrel. They went out too far ahead. The dogs seemed to have picked up a good bit of scent. Several times they went on point, but we'd advance to flush the bird and there was no bird there."

With a laugh I said "Well, they're pretty uncooperative rascals at times."

"How about you fellows," the general asked. "Did you do any good this morning?"

"Yes," I said. "We had a pretty successful morning."

"Scared up a few rabbits, did you?"

"Rabbits and birds," I replied.

"You're not hunting birds with that dog surely," he said, motioning toward Judy. "I never heard of such a thing."

I said "How about those short hairs. They any good?"

"Any good!" the general exclaimed rather indignantly.

"Why, I traveled all the way to Kansas to get those dogs. They're school trained and descended from a very coveted bloodline. I had to put my order in a year before they were born. I have ten generation pedigrees for them, and on top of all that they cost me a small fortune. Why, just a few weeks ago my brother and I took them to a Georgia plantation for a five day quail hunt. They exceeded my expectations. Of course they are any good!"

Just about the time the general finished his dissertation, Frank, who'd been taking all of this in said, "Hey Dad. A big cock bird just flew in and landed in that corn stubble field down there."

Looking downgrade from where we stood, I saw a long narrow field in which the corn had been cut.

"Where did he land?" I asked.

"Just about ten yards in from the near edge " Frank replied.

To the general I said, "Well, let's go for him. I'd like to see what those short hairs can do."

"Alright," said the general. "You're in for a good show. But, you'll have to hold your beagle back. She'll get in their way."

"Glad to," I said. "You and Frank go for the point. Judy and I will just stand back and watch."

We hastened to the spot where Frank had seen the bird land. As soon as we got there, Judy began to pick up the scent. She immediately began to bawl and tug at her leash, to the point where I was forced to lay my gun down and pick her up lest she back up and slip her collar.

The general, in the meantime, had summoned his dogs to the spot Frank had pointed out, and was giving them commands. Frank was standing at the ready with his thumb on his gun safety.

After perhaps ten minutes had passed, during which the short hairs had romped all over the place, the general said to Frank, "Son, are you sure you saw a bird land here?"

"I'm positive," Frank replied. Pointing to the exact spot he said, "He landed right there."

Scratching his head in frustration, the general said. "I don't understand it. Don't understand it."

By that time Judy had become next to impossible to control. "General," I said, "If we're ever going to find that pheasant, I'm going to have to turn this dog loose. The bird may be too far gone by now, but we'll give it a shot anyway."

"Alright," said the general reluctantly. "Let her go."

Before I turned her loose I said, "Now you're going to have to hold those "Mutts" back. They'll get in her way."

With Frank's help he grudgingly leashed his dogs.

I said, "Now general, this is a different ball game. You're going to have to run behind her and try to keep up until she gains on the bird and he flushes. You will be on one side, and Frank on the other. I'll stay put and hold onto your dogs."

"Oh, I'm not able to do that," he said. "You and the boy go ahead. I'll just stand here and watch."

Judy by this time was hysterical. The moment I released her, she was off in high gear on the pheasant's trail, bawling all the while. Frank and I were hard pressed to keep up.

"We'll be awfully lucky to get a shot, Frank," I said. "The bird's too far ahead by now. But let's give it our best try anyway."

There was a fence at the far end of the field with six inch by six inch openings between the wires. The pheasant didn't slow down at the fence, but slipped right through. Judy got caught up in the wires, but somehow she managed to wiggle free.

We were a good twenty yards behind her when she reached the fence, and by the time we got there I'd pretty well given up hope of getting a shot, but still we persisted.

"Here Dad," Frank said as he handed me his gun and quickly proceeded to climb over. When he reached the other side, I handed him both guns butt first through an opening. I then lifted Judy to the top, where Frank grabbed her and put her on the ground. I attempted then, to climb over the fence which was about five feet high.

On the opposite side was a pasture, and the grade sloped downward to a small stream forty to fifty yards ahead.

Just as I reached the top of the fence and was holding on to a post making ready to jump down on the opposite side, I looked toward the stream in time to watch the cock bird take to the air from the near stream bank. Judy, at that moment, was no more than ten yards behind him.

We laughed as Frank said, "Well Dad, we got a good workout anyway, even though we didn't get a shot."

"I really didn't think we would," I said. "We were too far behind when the chase got underway."

I jumped down on the cornfield side, and Frank passed the guns back through.

Judy, by that time, had come back to Frank. He praised her and gave her a treat, then lifted her to the top of the fence. I got hold of her and put her on the ground, and then Frank climbed over.

General O'Brien had, in the meantime, walked across the field to our position with his dogs leashed.

"I swear," he said, "I've never seen anything like that in my life. I had no idea those birds would run that far."

"Normally they won't," I said. "But I have, on a few occasions, seen them run farther than that."

"I still don't understand why these dogs wouldn't go on point," he said.

"Well, General," I replied, "I guess they wouldn't go on point simply because the bird wasn't there."

I went on to say, "I've only hunted over bird dogs a few times in my life, and in most cases it's been grouse hunting.

But on one occasion, I hunted pheasants with a friend who owned a good Springer Spaniel. The instant the spaniel picked up a scent, he'd make a wide circle to the front and box the bird in between him and shooter. Having no escape route on the ground, the bird would take to the air presenting an open shot.

But in my limited experience, I've never seen a ring-neck hold very long for a point."

"Looks like you fellows really work for those birds. I can't get over that. Wish I'd had a movie camera," he said.

"That's what makes it exciting," I replied. "It's well after lunch time. Let's go in and have a sandwich and see if we can get back out in time for another chase or two."

On our walk to the farmhouse, we fell into a pleasant conversation and traded a few stories as hunters are inclined to do.

When we reached the farmhouse, we took advantage of the beautiful fall day, and sat down outside to cool off and have a sandwich and a welcomed drink. Frank filled Judy's water bowl, and she proved to be plenty thirsty from her hard morning hunt.

Jean and Sam came out and joined us, and the General relayed a full account of the chase he'd seen. "I never realized those birds would run that far," he said.

Sam said "I've seen them scoot out ahead of my corn cutter into an open pasture and run like a deer clear to the other side."

As we finished our sandwiches, I said to Frank "Well, let's get on out there and see if we can scare something up. It's getting late."

Turning to the General I asked, "Would you care to join us?"

He laughed and replied "Thank you, but I think I've had enough for one day."

As he began to pack up for his trip home and we made ready to hunt for awhile, I said "General I'm glad we ran upon you today. Hope we get to see you again soon. I hope your dogs do well for you."

"I hope so," he said as we shook hands. "I'll remember the show you fellows and that little dog put on, for a long time."

With a smile I said, "I'm sure you will, and I'll bet we will too."

Judy worked up a hen and a cock bird before evening on that day. Frank put the cock bird down with his second shot.

She routed one more rabbit which I shot as it circled near me.

With complete satisfaction, we headed home that evening after another perfect day afield with Judy.

CHAPTER XII
THE PREACHER IN THE HONEYSUCKLE PATCH

The church which my family and I attended near our home in Virginia was presided over by an elderly minister, Dr. Andrew Watson. Dr. Watson had a young assistant, the Reverend Daniel Olson. Dr. Watson was active in the conference of churches and was called upon to speak at other churches regularly. On those occasions, Reverend Olson preached our Sunday sermons.

During the social hours following the Sunday services, Reverend Olson, who enjoyed outdoor sports, often came to Frank and me to hear the story of our previous day's adventure. He always listened attentively as we recounted our experiences which were highlighted by Judy's superior performance. Many times our discussions outlasted the social hour, and ended only by the urging of Alice and Mrs. Olson.

The Reverend said he owned a shotgun, and in his youth he'd hunted quail and doves with his father in the Carolinas where he grew up. He had shot at quail with bird dogs belonging to friends of his father, but had never hunted with a beagle.

One Sunday morning during the hunting season at the close of a particularly fascinating tale, the Reverend said, "That's amazing. How I'd love to have an experience like that."

I said, "Well, why don't you plan to hunt with us next Saturday? We'd be pleased to have you with us."

"Saturday is not a good day for me," he replied. "I usually have to do my final sermon preparation so that it will be fresh in my mind on the following day."

As it happened, I had accumulated many vacation days which I'd have to use by the end of the year. We selected a day in the following week which would be suitable to both our schedules, and made our plans for that day.

Frank was disappointed that he'd be in school and unable to be with us. But I reminded him that I had arranged with his principal for his week-long absence during the Pennsylvania deer season which was only a few weeks away, and I didn't think it was advisable for him to miss more school than that. Moreover, he and I would be hunting together on the following Saturday.

On the designated day, Reverend Olson arrived at our home just before daybreak as we'd planned. I had brought Judy into the house by that time, and she began to howl when he knocked at the door. They soon became friends as we loaded our gear and got underway.

Our destination that morning was a farm near Berryville, Virginia, which I'd obtained permission to hunt a year or two earlier, but had not yet hunted that year.

On that farm, there was a sparsely-wooded area consisting of a few acres, which had grown thick with an under-story of honeysuckle and briars. The patch was completely surrounded by lush farm fields, and had yielded plenty of rabbits during the previous season.

On our hour and a half trip, I explained a few things to the Reverend about hunting rabbits with beagles. Since this was to be a new experience for him, he had many questions. He found it somewhat hard to believe that when a rabbit was pursued by the dog, it would return to a spot near where it had been routed.

The sky was overcast that morning, with the temperature in the low forties. The barometric pressure suggested a storm may be gathering. I mentioned to the Reverend that under these conditions, the rabbit will often hole up when it's routed, but in small patches like the one we were about to hunt, they will usually run a short circle or two before they do.

We soon reached our destination. The honeysuckle patch began at a five-minute walk from the spot where I parked. I kept Judy leashed until we arrived there.

I suggested we spread out to allow twenty yards between us. I had explained on the trip what to do when Judy found a hot scent, but I reiterated that when her tail began to wag furiously, we'd stop and give her a chance to work it out.

When we reached the honeysuckle patch, I released Judy. The Reverend and I spread out and advanced into the cover.

We hadn't gone far when I noticed that Judy had found a hot scent. I motioned for the Reverend to stop and pointed to Judy. In a moment, she began to yip, then to bawl, and I knew the chase was on.

"Preacher," I said, "try quickly to get yourself in a position where you stand a chance for a reasonably open shot. Remain perfectly still, and keep your eyes peeled. Chances are, the rabbit will run a short circle in this cover and he won't be far ahead of the dog."

As I'd predicted, the rabbit hopped around in the cover briefly, then broke into a short circle toward the Reverend.

In a few moments, the Reverend raised his pump gun and quickly cranked off three wild shots.

I held my position as Judy continued to bawl. In a few more moments, I caught sight of the rabbit heading for a broadside shot, roughly twenty yards to my left front. As he came abreast, I dumped him with a single shot from my modified barrel.

"I don't know how I missed," said the Reverend. "I thought I was right on him."

"That's why you missed," I replied. "On a broadside shot you need to give him a lead, shoot where he's going to be when the shot gets there, not where he is now. The lead has to correspond to both his speed and how far the shot must travel."

I showed the Reverend how to field dress a rabbit. Then, Judy and I went about our success ritual with the affectionate praise and the liver treat.

The Reverend asked, "Won't that make her sick?"

"It never has," I said. "And I'm sure she's eaten at least one hundred of them by now. But, I limit it to three or four per day and I always take out the gall bladder."

Soon after we resumed our hunt, we got into some high briars and for a few minutes the Reverend was out of my sight. Soon, I heard him discharge another three shots in rapid succession.

"Did you get him?" I called.

"No," he said. "I just caught a glimpse of him as he ran out of a honeysuckle clump ahead of me."

I hurried over, asked him where he'd seen the rabbit, and called to Judy. She was already excited from the sound of the shots, and wasted no time getting there.

Putting my hand to the ground I said the old familiar, "There he goes, Judy. Find the bunny."

Off she went immediately, sounding off on the hot scent.

"Boy," said the Reverend. "What a well-trained dog."

"It's in her genes," I said. "And she's had lots of practice. Now, try to find a good shooting lane where you'll have a reasonable chance for an open shot. I'll move over to the right twenty-five yards or so."

The rabbit bounced around in the thick cover ahead of Judy for twenty minutes or so before he evened out in a circle. From Judy's position, I could tell that, just as the previous chase, this one was headed toward the Reverend. I hoped it would continue in that direction. Fearing he might get discouraged and lose interest, I really wanted him to score on this rabbit.

Soon, I heard the familiar three rapid shots. The rabbit made an abrupt left turn re-entering the dense cover, where he hopped back and forth for a good while. Not wanting to add insult to injury, I refrained from calling out, "Did you get him?"

Momentarily, Judy stopped bawling, and I thought he'd holed up. But in a moment she sounded off again and I knew that the chase was still on.

The rabbit circled to the right this time and headed toward my position. He appeared to be running toward me at the edge of the thicket. Just as I fired, he turned abruptly to re-enter the cover, with Judy close behind him.

As she continued into the dense cover, I thought I'd missed. But soon her howling ceased, and she emerged with the rabbit between her teeth, and laid him at my feet.

I called out, "I got him," and as I began to field dress the rabbit the Reverend joined me at my position, shaking his head.

"I just don't understand why I keep missing these rabbits," he said. "Why, I'm nearly out of ammunition."

Jokingly I said, "Preacher, where did you buy your ammunition, anyway?"

"At the sporting goods store, why?" he asked.

I said, "I think you should gather up your spent cartridges, take them back, tell them that they had no shot in them and demand a refund."

"Unfortunately," said the Reverend, "I can't blame it on the ammunition, or on anything else, for that matter, except my poor marksmanship."

"Preacher," I said, "might I give you a word of advice?"

"Please do," he answered.

I said, "I noticed each time you fired at a rabbit, you cranked off three rounds as fast as they could be chambered. In my observance, you're not focusing on that first shot. You're not following through with your sighting, or attaching enough importance to accuracy. Instead, you're blazing away with your pump gun, relying on the fact that you have two back-up shots. I've seen hunters do that on other occasions. As a boy, I found that one accurate shot is better than a thousand poorly placed ones."

"It stands to reason that you're right, but nonetheless it's discouraging to miss three times in a row," he replied.

I said, "Consider this: this is your first experience hunting rabbits with a dog. And how long has it been since you've fired a shotgun at anything?"

"It's been a few years," he replied.

"Well," I said, "don't be discouraged. You'll get the hang of it in due time. I've been doing this almost since I was in diapers, and I still miss a shot at times. Anyone who tells you he's never missed, either hasn't hunted much, or he's not telling the truth. A miss now and then is inevitable to all of us. It's just part of the turf and it keeps us humble. Are you really out of ammunition?"

"I have three shells left," he said.

Luckily, he was carrying the same gauge gun as I was, so I handed him a half dozen shells.

"I hate to take yours," he said. "What if you run out?"

"It's no problem," I answered. "I always keep an extra box or two in the car. Besides, these have shot in them."

We had a good laugh and then went back to the thicket. We hadn't even begun to cover it and already we'd bagged three rabbits. There was an exceptionally high concentration of rabbits there, and the reason for it was obvious. The surrounding lush crop fields provided an excellent feed source right next to the protective dense honeysuckle and briar cover.

We hadn't gone far until Judy sounded off on another chase. As the rabbit circled to the right, I caught sight of it in the briars. In the hope that it would continue to the Reverend's position, I did not shoot.

Soon, I heard him fire a single shot. In a few moments I called out, "Did you get him?"

"I don't think so," he replied.

I reached his position at about the same time as Judy showed up, still bawling on the trail.

"Where was he when you shot?" I asked.

"He was just ahead of where Judy is now, heading into those dense briars. I thought I was going to get a good broadside shot, but he must have seen me raise my gun, because he turned sharply to the left and went for the briars. After I fired I could no longer see him."

"Let's just wait and see what Judy does," I said, with a pretty good idea of what had happened.

In a moment Judy's howling ceased. In a few more moments, out of the briars she trotted, proudly holding the Preacher's rabbit aloft.

I shook the Reverend's hand and congratulated him on his first rabbit.

"I'd never have found him without Judy," he said.

"It often happens that way," I replied. "This cover seems to be alive with rabbits, but as dense as it is, we'd be hard-pressed to find one without a good dog."

Over a sandwich, we critiqued the morning hunt, replenished our ammunition, and made plans to hit the cover for another hour or two in the afternoon. The Reverend's successful shot noticeably stimulated his enthusiasm.

During the afternoon, Judy routed three more rabbits. The Reverend missed the first one, and it holed at mid-point of the second circle. He made a direct hit on the second, and I scored on the third.

As I stowed the third rabbit I said, "That's about enough game to take from this patch in one day. I think we should leave a few for seed. Have you had enough for one day?"

"Yes," he said, "but I want you to know this has been the most enjoyable day I've had for a very long time. I'll have to admit I was a little discouraged after all those misses, but the moment I saw Judy carrying that rabbit out of the briars I regained my enthusiasm. I want you to know how much I appreciate your invitation."

Our homeward route passed through the town of Leesburg, Virginia. I decided to stop for a brief visit with one of my very closest, and most respected, lifelong friends, Joe Pesi. Joe and his wife, Betty, reside in the beautiful home which they themselves created, two miles west of the city limits.

For most of our lives, Joe and Betty have been very special people to my family and me. We've shared many happy times together, and they've given us unlimited support through some very trying times.

Joe and I have hunted and fished together for more than half a century. My son Frank III, who adored Joe, accompanied us on many trips. Frank was deeply influenced by Joe's wisdom, his sound advice, and his benevolent nature.

I had planned to give some of our rabbits to Joe and Betty, but Betty declined the offer. She didn't like to cook them, she said, since they were full of BBs and hair.

While sharing a most welcomed cup of hot coffee and Betty's homemade cookies, the Reverend recounted the events of our hunt in the honeysuckle patch. Joe and Betty were enlightened and amused by his story, and by the enthusiasm with which he told it.

On the remainder of our short journey home, the Reverend repeated what a splendid day he'd had, and thanked me again for taking him along.

"My pleasure," I said. "Before the season ends we'll try to do it again."

At our social hour on the following Sunday morning, Reverend Olson drew a sizable audience as he relayed in nearly every detail the story of our day's hunt during the previous week.

He described the lay of the land, and the reasons I'd given him that the patch had potential. He told of how he'd missed with his shots until he began to focus on the rabbits, and tried to make his first shot count. He admitted that he'd been hard-pressed to believe me when, prior to the hunt, I'd explained that the rabbit would circle back to the hunter ahead of the dog.

His special emphasis however, and the aspect of the hunt he'd remember the longest, was the outstanding performance of our great gun dog, Judy.

CHAPTER XIII
GIVING BACK

As I mentioned at the beginning of this story, I spent my childhood and formative years in the home of my paternal grandparents where my Aunt Lois and Uncle Pat raised me as their own.

After my mother's death, my father Dr. Frank Deter, Sr. remained in Ohio in his position as a high school principal and superintendent. He served in that capacity until the outbreak of World War II, when he entered the United States Army.

Throughout the war years, he served as an intelligence officer. He re-married prior to the end of the war, and within a year my delightful little sister was born and named after my aunt, Lois Endean Deter.

At the end of the war, Dad resigned from active Army duty. With his new family, he re-established himself in Central Tennessee, and became Director of Psychology at a large Veteran's Administration Hospital. He taught classes in psychology at three universities. He founded the Tennessee Chapter of the American Psychological Association and served as it's president for many years.

After his retirement, he founded the Rutherford County Guidance Center, and presided over it until in his later years he became incapacitated by failing health.

During my boyhood years, Dad came to the old home place in Reynoldsville as often as his circumstances allowed. On those occasions he, Uncle Pat, and I shared many great hunting and fishing adventures, often in the company of relatives and old friends.

After my family and I became established in our home in Virginia, Dad came for a week-long visit each year when his schedule permitted. At an opportune time during that week, he and I drove to the old Pennsylvania home and spent a few days with his sister, Aunt Lois.

Like myself, Dad had been a hunter and gun dog enthusiast from a very early age. During most of his years in Tennessee, he had owned thoroughbred beagles. Organizer that he was, he drew together a group of colleagues and friends who shared his interest. Rabbits were very plentiful in that part of Tennessee, and he and his friends enjoyed many years of good hunting.

On several occasions during my Marine Corps years while stationed in the Carolinas, I drove to his home and joined him on some very exciting and productive hunts.

From the time my son and I began to hunt with Judy and I relayed the tales of our adventures to him, Dad expressed his wish to join us. Dedicated to his profession as he was, he never could seem to afford time during the hunting seasons to make the seven hundred mile trip and be there at a convenient time for a hunt.

By the time Judy became six or seven years old, Dad began to feel the initial effects of Parkinson's disease. We knew of course, that the affliction was incurable and would gradually worsen as time passed.

While he found it difficult to acknowledge that foreboding, I was able to convince him that we should no longer postpone our hunt. He should plan his yearly visit to coincide with the Pennsylvania small game season. Judy would accompany us on our visit with Aunt Lois, and we would spend our long overdue day afield in the vicinity of our boyhood home.

Dad found every aspect of my proposal favorable. He quickly went about arranging for his work at the guidance center to continue during his absence and began to prepare for the trip.

Our trip to Reynoldsville had become an event that I anxiously looked forward to each year. It gave us the opportunity to catch up on each other's activities during the previous year. We reminisced about our adventures together in years gone by, and discussed plans for years yet to come. We talked about our fishing trips, on many of which my son, Frank III had accompanied us.

Dad was a very wise and profound man. He never ceased to have words of advice which I always found beneficial in time to come.

When I told my son Frank III about the plans Dad and I had made, he was disappointed that he could not accompany us, as he always loved sharing experiences with his Granddad. However, by that time he was in high school and the trip would coincide with the time to prepare for mid-term examinations. Moreover, I had already arranged for his absence from school during deer season.

Soon, the time arrived and we met Dad at the airport. After a few days during which he visited with Alice and the kids; he, Judy, and I departed for Reynoldsville. By the time we reached our destination, he and Judy had become well acquainted and good friends.

When we arrived at our destination, I gave Dad time to spend with Aunt Lois while I began to make final preparations for our hunt.

One of my favorite uncles (through marriage), Raymond Krushevsky, whom I referred to as "Uncle Peanuts" lived in Reynoldsville. Peanuts had taken me hunting on many occasions when I was a boy. In fact, he had taken me deer hunting on that memorable day when I shot my first buck at age thirteen. Like Dad and myself, he was a life long gun dog enthusiast, and had owned many thoroughbred beagles. He was near Dad's age at that time and like Dad, was in failing health. Like nearly everyone else in the old home town, he referred to me as "Nickie."

I called Uncle Peanuts and invited him to join us for a hunt. He was overjoyed with the invitation and the opportunity to hunt with my Dad and me once again. But, he reminded me that he was no longer able to pound the thickets as aggressively as he had in the past. He and I had communicated regularly over the years and I had recounted many of our experiences with Judy. He said "I'll be anxious to see what that magic dog of yours can do."

Dad was delighted that Peanuts would be joining us, since they were old friends and had not hunted together for many years. Both these men were life long beaglers and knew the drill as well, or perhaps better, than I did. I knew however, that due to their age and physical condition, much consideration on my part would be required.

I knew of a sizeable farm in that vicinity which had been sold to a coal company and abandoned several years earlier. The fields had grown up with swale grass, golden rods and sparse briars, but had not yet become so dense that a rabbit hunt should be too strenuous.

Early on the morning of the hunt, Dad, Judy, and I proceeded to Peanuts' home on the other side of town. Peanuts was eagerly awaiting us, with his game coat and his old 16 gauge double in hand.

On our way to the farm, Judy displayed her normal hunting day excitement, leaping from front to back in the car and occasionally sounding off with a howl. I described the farm to my companions and told them not to tire themselves out pounding the cover, but to let Judy and me do the work. "If there are rabbits there," I said, "she'll find them."

"She certainly seems anxious to hunt," Peanuts said. "How's her endurance?"

"Remarkable," I said. "Just like everything else about her."

In perhaps twenty minutes, we arrived at the hunting ground. I pulled in where an overgrown field bordered the road. I kept Judy on the leash until we planned our strategy and loaded up.

The sky was overcast that morning with the temperature in the thirties. There had been flurries the previous night, and the ground was covered with a very thin blanket of snow.

When we'd fallen into position twenty yards abreast, I released Judy who was anxiously straining at her leash. I had taken the center position, with Dad on my left and Peanuts on my right. The purpose was to keep both of them in sight, and present each of them with an opportunity for a shot when Judy or I bounced a rabbit.

We hadn't progressed far into the field when I began to see fresh rabbit tracks in the snow. "There are rabbit tracks here," I called to the others.

Ten yards ahead Judy's tail was wagging and she was sniffing pretty hard. "She's cold trailing," I said. "She'll likely pick up a hot one soon."

A little farther on, Judy's tail began to wag more quickly, and as she entered a small briar patch she began the yip which soon gave way to her bawl.

"Music to my ears," said Peanuts as he repositioned himself to a better field of view. "What a beautiful voice."

"Dad," I called. "Do you have a good shooting lane?"

"I'm good," he said.

The rabbit ran farther out ahead than I expected it to, then began to make a wide circle to the right. At the right edge of the field, the terrain sloped upward into a large wooded area. By Judy's voice, I could tell that the rabbit had penetrated deeply into the woods.

Peanuts called to me, "Nickie, I don't think that rabbit's going to circle this far back. We should move ahead forty yards or so and swing our firing line to the right.

"I think your right," I said. "Dad," I called. "Let's move ahead and swing to the right before he comes out of that woods. You take the left flank, let Peanuts have the center, and I'll hang back on the right just in case he does try to double back."

By the time we re-aligned our position, I could tell that the rabbit was headed back toward the field. From where I stood I could see Peanuts, but I couldn't see Dad. Peanuts however, had given me a thumbs up, meaning we were all at the ready.

In perhaps five minutes I heard Dad fire a single shot from his pump gun. When he called out "I got him," Peanuts and I hastened to his position, where we all waited until Judy finished her chase.

With her usual procedure, when Judy came upon the rabbit she picked it up and shook it a few times, laid it at our feet and proudly looked up at me. I picked her up, made quite a fuss over her, and gave her a treat.

"What a terrific chase!" Dad said.

"She never missed a beat," Peanuts added. "On a chase that long it's a rare dog that won't over-run a turn and stop sounding off a few times at least. But, she held to that scent the entire time."

As we field dressed, stowed the rabbit, and gave Judy her liver treat, we discussed our strategy for continuing the morning's hunt. I'd hoped to avoid taking Dad and Peanuts into heavy cover where our movement would be strenuous.

With that purpose in mind I said, "I think we should stick to these overgrown fields. There's plenty of good feed and cover in them and my guess is the rabbits stuck to heavy cover during last night's squalls, and they'll be feeding in the fields throughout the morning."

"We taught you well Nickie," said Peanuts. "You can bet your boots that's just what they're doing."

We started out again in our same line-up, with Judy directly ahead of my center position.

When we'd proceeded perhaps seventy-five yards, I could tell by Judy's motions that she was picking up another hot scent. I alerted Dad and Peanuts, and we slowed our pace with guns at the ready.

In front of my position, the tall weeds gave way somewhat to a sparse stand of briars and I was able to see for a good distance ahead.

Soon, Judy began to yip as she entered the briars. In a moment, I saw a rabbit bounce out ahead of her. She saw the rabbit and immediately began to bawl as she took up the chase. When she'd gone about ten yards, I caught a glimpse of a second rabbit as it scooted off to the left. In only a moment, I saw a third one peel off to the right.

When both the second and the third rabbits were routed and Judy turned her head, I knew she'd seen both of them. But, she did not break her pace from the chase she had started.

I called to Dad and Peanuts, who by that time had gotten into positions with a field of view. "Watch out ahead," I said. "There are three rabbits out."

"Three?" Peanuts asked. "Are you sure?"

"I saw them," I said.

"Which one is she chasing?" Dad asked.

"The first one," I replied.

With about a normal length circle, Judy brought the rabbit around to Peanuts, who scored on the first shot. I quickly walked over toward his position, and arrived there at about the end of the chase.

Judy finished her chase, laid the rabbit at our feet, then turned and headed back through the weeds.

Peanuts asked, "Where's she going?"

"She's going for one of those other rabbits," I replied, as I made my way back to my position.

I called to Dad, who'd begun to walk toward Peanuts, "Stay in your position Dad," I said. "She's going for one of those other rabbits."

No sooner had I spoken, than Judy began to bawl. After a circle of about the same duration as the previous one, Judy's voice told me that the chase was headed in Peanuts' direction once again. In a short time, I heard the report of Peanuts' gun. After a brief pause, he touched off his second barrel, after which he called out "I got him. I winged him with the first shot and finished him with the second."

Judy soon finished the chase, laid the rabbit at Peanuts' feet, and hastened back into the weeds.

Peanuts called to me, "She's headed back into the weeds again. You don't think she's going for that third rabbit, do you?"

"Yes I do," I replied.

"I can't believe it," he said.

"Dad," I called, "Keep your position. She's not finished yet."

"Well I declare," he said.

The third chase turned out to be a rather long one, so we all moved ahead thirty to forty yards. Once again,

Judy never missed a beat and after twenty minutes or so, I could tell that the rabbit was circling to the left and hopefully would soon come into Dad's field of view.

In a few minutes, I heard the single shot I was hoping for, after which Dad called out, "I got him."

When I reached Dad's position and found him grinning from ear to ear I said, "You're still a pretty good shot old boy. Two shots for two rabbits."

Uncle Peanuts arrived there carrying his two rabbits and shaking his head at about the same time as Judy wound up the third chase. "I wouldn't believe it if I hadn't seen it," he said. "I've owned some pretty good dogs in my time, but I've never seen one perform like that before."

My Dad, always the professor regardless of where he was, stood almost at attention with his forefinger extended as he proclaimed, "Son, that is a phenomenal gun dog. It's unfortunate that you haven't run her in field trials."

Peanuts added, "She'd have taken the Blue Ribbon every time."

When Judy completed the chase, I picked her up and hugged her, and we all made quite a fuss over her performance. I put her on the leash and tied it to a sapling so she wouldn't start another chase before we finished field dressing the three rabbits. She laid down and looked up as if to say, "I think I'm due for a break." I gave her two livers which made a total of three, and which I felt was enough for one day.

As we finished dressing out the rabbits, I looked at my watch. It was getting near noon. I said to Dad and Peanuts, "It's near noon. We have three options and I'll let the decision up to the two of you. If you're tired out we can call it a day now. Or, we can go somewhere and have a bite of lunch, and come back out this afternoon. For the third option we can skip lunch and go for another chase or two now and call it quits in mid-afternoon. What'll it be gentlemen?"

"Well son," Dad said "My legs are telling me that I've had enough, but I'd really love to see that little dog run another rabbit or two before we quit."

"What about you Uncle Peanuts? Are you good for another hour or two?" I asked.

"Like your Dad said, my old bones are telling me it's near quitting time, and if I knock off for lunch I know I won't get started again today. But, I'd really like to see Judy make one more chase," he replied.

"Okay then," I said. "We'll give it a go for another hour or so, then we'll pack it in. I'm sure there are more rabbits in these fields, so there's no need to climb any hills or wade through dense cover. Moreover, we don't need to be in any hurry. Let Judy range out and find the rabbits. If you see that it's too much for you, tell me and we'll quit."

I unleashed Judy, and we moved out toward another large field with similar cover. I was a bit concerned for Dad and Peanuts, since they both appeared somewhat worse for wear. But, I knew what it meant to these lifelong hunters to see one more good chase. I also knew to my deep regret, that this in all likelihood would be the last rabbit hunt for both of them.

Judy ran two more rabbits on that day. The first one holed up after a short run. The second was a beautiful chase which ended with a single shot from my modified barrel.

By then, the time was approaching 2:00 P.M. So, I said to my companions, "Let's call it a day now. By the time we get home it will be past 2:30. Anyway, as both of you taught me many years ago, it's a good idea to leave a few for seed."

When we arrived at Uncle Peanuts' home, Aunt Sue had a pot of hot homemade soup waiting for us. Over lunch many hunting stories from years gone by were told. I remembered some of the hunts we talked about. Some had taken place before my time. Both Dad and Peanuts asked if I remembered certain dogs they'd owned when I was a boy. And indeed, I did remember them. Their names were etched in my mind.

I asked Aunt Sue to call Aunt Lois and let her know we'd returned from the hunt, so that I wouldn't be scolded for overexerting Dad and Peanuts.

Our little Judy soon gained the forefront of the conversation. Neither of my elders could seem to say enough about her performance with those three rabbits. In all of their years afield, neither of them had ever seen a feat like that before. Nor had I, of course.

Both of them had heard the story of my attempt to have Judy bred. The fact that they both were well acquainted with the beagle authorities, Friz Harmon and Calvin Becker, once again made the story all the more laughable.

Finally Peanuts asked, "Nickie why don't you try again to have her bred? In just a few years she's going to start slowing down. I'll be surprised if you'll ever have another one like her, but your best chance is with one of her own pups."

"He's absolutely right, son," Dad said. "Your prospect of ever finding another dog that can approach her performance is highly unlikely."

"Well," I said "I have given it some thought, but there's much to consider. First of all, I'd rather not put Judy or myself through another ordeal like the last time. I thought for awhile both Calvin and Friz would have heart attacks."

That being said, everyone including, Aunt Sue, had another good laugh.

I went on to say, "By the time Judy's no longer able to hunt my son will be beginning his adult life, and I'll be looking forward to retirement and relocation. At the present time, I'm considering the purchase of rural property in North Central Pennsylvania and settling there when the time comes. So, there will be a transition period of a few years, during which I'll have little time for hunting and running dogs. After I'm resettled, I'm sure I'll have more dogs and I'll have the opportunity to devote more time to hunting."

We gave Peanuts and Sue all of the rabbits. They insisted we should take some with us, but I reminded them that we were in transit, and not in a position to keep them.

In parting, Uncle Peanuts said, "I really appreciate it, Nickie. I can't remember when I had such a thoroughly enjoyable day."

"The pleasure's been entirely mine," I said. "Hope to see you again soon."

After a few days visit with Aunt Lois and with old friends and acquaintances, Dad, Judy and I left for our journey back to Virginia. As always, with Dad's company and many words of wisdom, it was a delightful drive.

On the following day, I drove Dad to the airport for his flight to Tennessee. On the way there he said, "Son, I want you to know how eternally grateful I am for what you did. The opportunity for us to hunt together again in the company of an old friend will be treasured in my memory. And, the privilege and delight of hunting with that astounding little dog exceeded my expectations by far."

"Dad," I said, "Believe me the privilege and the pleasure of hunting with you once again was entirely mine."

As we parted on that day, I was saddened with the realization that Dad and I had just shared our last day afield together. In the ensuing months, his condition deteriorated rapidly. Within a year, his affliction with Parkinson's disease and the side effects of his medication would render him nearly totally incapacitated, requiring constant care.

Uncle Peanuts, as fate would have it, had also spent his last day tramping the woods and fields. He would soon lose nearly all the strength in his legs and his heart condition would rapidly worsen.

Alone with my thoughts as I drove home that day, many treasured experiences from the past came to mind. I thought of the countless occasions when both Dad and Uncle Peanuts had taken me hunting and fishing, taught me many priceless lessons, and had done so much for my well-being.

I was intensely grateful for the opportunity and the privilege of taking them on their last hunt, and looking out for their safety and well-being as they had done for me so many times, so long ago. It was the satisfying and rewarding feeling of giving something back, even if by comparison it was very small.

I was especially thankful for our outstanding gun dog Judy, who made their day to a much greater extent than I had, and had made the memory of their final hunt everlasting.

CHAPTER XIV
JUDY'S LAST HUNT

As the years passed, my son and I continued to enjoy countless hours combing the fields and thickets with Judy in the lead.

When the scarlet and gold leaves began to rustle in the crisp autumn breeze, and the squirrels in our yard began to store their winter cache, our thoughts always turned once again to the approaching hunting seasons.

We continued to take Judy to the training grounds a time or two each week. Not because she required additional training, but because we wanted to provide her with the opportunity to do what she loved and was born to do.

Among the local outdoorsmen and at our sportsman's club, Judy's reputation continued to broaden and became the subject of many conversations. Consequently, many friends and acquaintances sought to hunt with her, and on occasions we invited one or two to join us.

When Judy became seven or eight years old she had begun to show her age somewhat, and began to settle down considerably. She no longer jumped from seat to seat in the car, nor did she romp through the house so impatiently on the morning of a hunt. She did however, continue to serenade the neighbors on those mornings. As yet her age had little adverse effect on her skills and endurance, and she continued to maintain her determination and aggressiveness on the hunt.

Frank and I began to enjoy the late Pennsylvania season in particular. The weather was much cooler than in the early season, and neither hunter nor dog became over-heated nor tired as quickly. The high weeds had been beaten down from the winter storms by then, which enhanced the hunter's visibility. Often, the ground would be covered with snow, but in the southern tier of Pennsylvania where we usually hunted, the snow was normally light as opposed to the heavy snows of the north.

Judy seemed to love the snow. Where we normally hunted it was usually dense wet snow, unlike the dry powder of the north. Therefore, game scent lingered and was readily detected. From the hunters standpoint, it was helpful to see fresh tracks in the snow, indicating the presence of game.

While hunting the McNabb farm, we always kept a watchful eye for the little black and white sire of Judy's puppies. But, we never saw him again.

By the time Judy reached the age of ten or eleven and had begun to show her age very noticeably, Frank had grown to manhood and entered the United States Navy. He often told me how grateful he was for the many memorable experiences he had shared with Judy and me. He was now a dyed -in -the -wool hunter and gun dog enthusiast, and when he became established in life he hoped to have beagles of his own.

For another year or so, I continued to take Judy to the hunting and training grounds. While she maintained her eagerness, a gradual decline in her endurance was obvious. But, I felt that she had enriched Frank's life and my own to the extent that so long as she possessed the will to hunt, I was obligated to give her the opportunity.

When she reached the point where she seemed to require a long rest at the end of a chase, I limited our hunts to no more than a half-day. Remarkably, after she'd rested she'd get on her feet and make her way back to the cover.

One evening during the Pennsylvania hunting season, when Judy was nearly twelve years old, Alice said to me, "Your surely not going to take Judy hunting on Saturday, are you? She's too old now and I don't think she's able. We'd all feel terrible if something happened to her."

"Well," I said, "as long as she wants to go I feel I should take her."

When that Saturday morning came, she didn't make her usual hunting day fuss. As I approached her kennel she walked out of her shelter and stretched and yawned.

I said "Judy, shall we go hunting?" She yawned again and looked up with a rather sad expression. I lifted her out of the kennel and put her on the ground. When she looked up again I said, "Well, old girl, what's it going to be. Shall we go find a bunny?" When she heard the word "bunny" she began to whine, her tail began to wag and she ran to the fence gate as fast as her tired little legs could carry her.

I lifted her into the car, and as I gathered and stowed my gear Alice came out, petted her and said, "Don't you keep her out too long now. She's just not up to it."

"We'll be back in the early afternoon," I said. "But I have to give her this one last hunt."

Thinking it was best not to take her into dense cover, I decided to limit our hunt to the fields. She attempted to range out in front of me, as she always had, but soon she was just walking along at my heels, attempting to keep up with my pace.

In perhaps an hour I sat down on a big rock at the edge of a field, put her on my lap and gently petted her.

I said, " Looks like you've had about enough, old pal. I guess we'd better head for home."

As she looked into my eyes, there was little doubt in my mind that she understood and resigned herself that after all those years as an outstanding gun dog, her days afield had come and gone.

I decided to take a short cut through a sparsely wooded area for an easy walk back to the car. By then, Judy had tired to the point where she simply followed behind me. Halfway through the wooded area, I stepped over a large diameter fallen log. In a moment I heard Judy whimpering behind me in a futile attempt to cross the log. Sadly, I took her in my arms and carried her for the remainder of the walk.

Alice was anxiously awaiting our return on that day. She immediately came to check on Judy's condition as I turned into the driveway. She was greatly relieved with Judy's response to her affection. She prepared food and water as I carried Judy to her kennel. She said, "Now don't you take her to the woods anymore. She's had her day and she's had enough."

"You're right," I said and I relayed our morning's experience to her.

Throughout the following year, we extended every possible effort to see that Judy was comfortable and contented during her retirement. On weekends and evenings, we lifted her from her kennel to walk about leisurely, and sniff at the scent left by squirrels as they crossed our yard. When she tired, she went to her favorite napping place on our porch, where Alice had placed a rug for her comfort. When old friends with whom she'd hunted came to visit, she greeted them cheerfully.

On one occasion when I went to the backyard, Judy was not to be found. When I discovered that someone had inadvertently let the fence gate open I hastened to tell Alice, and she and I began to scour the neighborhood in search. By that time, Judy's eyesight and hearing were failing, and we were concerned that she would not be able to find her way home.

When to our relief Alice discovered her in a neighbor's yard sniffing at the ground, she seemed overjoyed that we'd found her and were taking her home.

Then one morning in the early fall of her thirteenth year, as I approached her kennel, I found Judy's lifeless body lying at the entrance to her shelter.

It was a very sad and tearful time for our entire family. As in the case of all our aged and failing loved ones, we come to resign ourselves to their eminent passing. But when the time comes, we find that we're never fully prepared.

Alice, Patsy and I communicated with Frank often, and I'd kept him informed concerning Judy's status. But when I told him of her passing, quite understandably, he was overcome with sadness. After all, he had grown up with Judy and over the years an intense bond had developed between them.

With Alice's help, I laid Judy to rest in a special place where many flowers grew. We agreed that Judy's years with us had provided a happy and memorable chapter in our lives. She had enriched our lives immeasurably from her first hunt until her last, and well beyond.

CHAPTER XV
REFLECTIONS

Many years have come and gone since Judy's passing. Frank and Patsy grew to maturity, were married, and have established lives of their own They each gave us a fine grandson and we became joyful grandparents.

As we'd planned, Alice and I purchased our rural property in north central Pennsylvania. Twelve years thereafter we retired and re-established ourselves there far from the fast pace of the city, with abundant outdoor sports opportunities at our doorstep.

My work became increasingly demanding and my limited spare time was consumed by my effort to develop and improve our Pennsylvania property. Therefore, I did not acquire another gun dog until we re-located.

I never hunted small game at the McNabb farm again. However, our friendship with Sam and Jean continued, and I hunted deer there a number of times. On most of those occasions, I took the time to walk to the place where Frank had shot his first rabbit. The events of that memorable day were so vivid in my mind that I could almost see them happening once again. As I listened in the wind, in my imagination I could once again hear little Judy's bawl as she pushed the rabbit to the waiting young hunter.

On that day and in that place, my son heard the mythical hunter's horn, which I hoped would draw him to the forests and fields many times in years to come.

During our remaining years in Virginia, I often went to the place where Alice and I had laid Judy to rest and contemplated our wonderful experiences.

On many evenings when I felt the need for relief and revitalization from a taxing day, I went for a walk at Judy's old training ground. While on my walk, that exciting day when Patsy and I witnessed Judy's first chase was always present in my thoughts.

Seldom has the day gone by over the years on which I haven't been mindful of how fortunate I was to have chosen a puppy destined to become that exceptional gun dog sought after by every beagler, but so rarely emerges from the breed.

It's given me great satisfaction to know that I attained the goal I'd set forth so many years ago when my son took his first steps afield as a licensed hunter. Through my good fortune, I was able to provide him with that once in a lifetime rare gun dog and treasured friend.

As I've mentioned, my family and I owned many beagles before Judy came into our lives. I've owned others since we came to live in the country. Some were mediocre or average, and some were quite astute hunters. But I can honestly say without hesitation, that no dog in the memory of my lifelong hunting experience can begin to measure up to our beloved Judy.

ACKNOWLEDGMENTS

I wish to express sincere appreciation to the following named persons whose dedicated assistance and support, and their tireless efforts greatly enhanced my ability to produce this book.

To my dear, faithful wife, Alice, who painstakingly typed every word, and provided considerable input concerning the content.

To my lovely daughter, Patsy, who provided inspiration, encouragement, and advice pertaining to the details of the story.

To Kayla Deter, wife of my grandson Frank Deter IV, who assisted greatly with computer technology.

To Kasey Cox, my editor, and co-owner of From My Shelf Books and Gifts, in Wellsboro, Pennsylvania. In addition to editing, Kasey provided unlimited advice for the preparation and publication of a book.

To Barbara Slocum, who proofread my manuscript and indicated the potential for cleaner copy in many cases.

To Marcia Welch, my graphic designer, who prepared the cover, and assisted significantly with the interior graphics and photographs.

To my dear son, Frank III, and to all those relatives, and friends who shared the many memorable experiences recounted herein.

Frank Deter, Jr.

Frank, daughter Patsy, Molly, & Judy III

THE AUTHOR

Frank Deter, Jr. grew up in the hill country of northwest Pennsylvania, where hunting and beagle ownership were a way of life. From his early boyhood he and his family owned and hunted with beagles.

As a young man Frank left home to serve in the United States Marine Corp, after which he pursued a career in Architecture, Engineering, Urban/Regional Planning and Landscape Contracting in the Washington D. C. vicinity.

Upon retirement in 1995, Frank and his wife Alice returned to the Pennsylvania hills where they reside at their country home to this day.

Since retirement, Frank has been active in tree farming, forest management and community service. With his continued passion for outdoor sports, he's hunted and fished on five continents.

A Dog Named Judy, true in every detail with exception of name substitutions, is the life story of a very exceptional thoroughbred beagle. As well as an outstanding gun dog, Judy was a beloved friend, companion, and family member. She will live eternally in the memories and in the hearts of Frank and his family and all others who shared the privilege of following her through forests and fields.